For the One
Voices from The One Project

For the One
Voices from The One Project

Edited by Nathan Brown with Alex Bryan and Japhet De Oliveira

Printed and published by
SIGNS PUBLISHING
Victoria, Australia

Copyright © 2014 by The One Project (Andrews University).
Copyright of the individual essays remains with the respective authors.

The authors assume full responsibility for the accuracy of all facts and quotations as cited in this book.

"Primal Adventism: Jesus at our beginning" is adapted from *The Green Cord Dream* by Alex Bryan (2012). Reprinted by permission of Pacific Press Publishing Association.

"A quarterback and a coach went up to the temple to pray . . ." is adapted from *Are you More Spiritual than a Fifth-grader? A Father and his Daughter Share the Timeless Teaching of Morris Venden* by Karl and Claire Haffner (2013). Reprinted by permission of Pacific Press Publishing Association.

Illustrations "The Way of Life" and "Christ, The Way of Life" (pages 46 and 47), reproduced by permission of Ellen G White Estate, Inc.

Proudly published and printed in Australia by
Signs Publishing
Warburton, Victoria.

This book was
Edited by Nathan Brown
Proofread by Lindy Schneider and Nathan Brown
Cover design by Ashlea Malycha
Typeset in Berkeley Book 11/14.5

ISBN (print edition) 978 1 921292 97 2
ISBN (ebook edition) 978 1 921292 98 9

"And the Word became flesh and dwelt among us, and we have seen his glory, glory as of the only Son from the Father, full of grace and truth" (John 1:14).

Unless otherwise indicated, all Bible quotations are taken from *The Holy Bible, English Standard Version*, copyright © 2001 by Crossway, a publishing ministry of Good News Publishers. All rights reserved.

Scripture quotations marked "KJV" are taken from the *Holy Bible, Authorised Version*.

Scripture quotations marked "NASB" are taken from the *New American Standard Bible*, copyright © 1960, 1962, 1963, 1968, 1971, 1972, 1973, 1975, 1977, 1995 by The Lockman Foundation. Used by permission.

Scripture quotations marked "NIV" are taken from the *Holy Bible, New International Version*, copyright © 1973, 1978 by the International Bible Society. Used by permission of Zondervan Bible Publishers.

Scripture quotations marked "NKJV" are taken from the *New King James Version*. Copyright © 1982 by Thomas Nelson, Inc. Used by permission. All rights reserved.

Scripture quotations marked "NLT" are taken from the *Holy Bible, New Living Translation*, copyright © 1996, 2004. Used by permission of Tyndale House Publishers, Inc., Wheaton, Illinois 60189. All rights reserved.

Scripture quotations marked "NRSV" are taken from the *New Revised Standard Version Bible*, copyright © 1989 the Division of Christian Education of the National Council of the Churches of Christ in the United States of America. Used by permission. All rights reserved.

Contents

Jesus. All. Introducing The One Project
    —Japhet De Oliveira 1
For the One Introducing this book*—Nathan Brown* 5

Jesus in Our History

Jesus Our identity, our mission and our song*—Tim Gillespie* 11
They Heard a Voice Jesus in our story*—Sam Leonor* 20
Primal Adventism Jesus at our beginning*—Alex Bryan* 26
The Forgotten Legacy of 1844 Jesus in our disappointment
    —Lisa Clark Diller. 36
"An unutterable yearning" Why 1888 matters
    to Adventists today*—Sam Leonor* 45
Deep Water Being amazed by Jesus*—Emily Whitney* 52

Jesus in Our Theology

Jesus. Doctrine. Jesus and our beliefs*—Mark Witas* 61
What is One? Jesus' prayer for unity*—Brandy Kirstein* 68
**"A quarterback and a coach went up to the
    temple to pray . . ."***—Karl Haffner* 78
Jesus. Wow. Recognizing Jesus as Lord*—Stephan Sigg* 89
A Second Touch Re-discovering Jesus*—Randy Roberts* 98
Phylacteries Celebrate, remember, love*—David Franklin* 107
The Heresy Response Jesus our Content*—Tim Gillespie* 117

Jesus in Our Practice

Jesus Rabbi. Healer. Chronicler. Rebel.*—Dilys Brooks* 127

Hens and Chicks The leadership of Jesus—*Timothy Nixon* 137
Cross-shaped Faith Jesus in our experience—*Terry Swenson* . . . 145
Trusting God, Washing Feet Jesus and
 practicing reconciliation—*Lisa Clark Diller* 152
Living Jesus Jesus and our ministry—*Eddie Hypolite* 159
"Thy Kingdom Come" Living Jesus' kingdom today
 —*Joanna Darby* 167

The One Project blessing 177

About the contributors 179

Jesus. All.

Introducing

The One Project

Japhet De Oliveira

Everything in my life was called into question. My dreams shattered. My hopes squashed. My energy depleted. I had lost my "super powers" of invincibility. I really never thought I would have had to face the dreaded C-word—"cancer." I had surgery to remove my thyroid, followed by a blast of radiation that re-set my clock. If I do not die within the next 50 years from something else, the cancer will come back and wipe me out.

This experience threw me into a spiral of complex questions and scenarios. *What if you knew you would die tomorrow? What video messages would you record for your family? Who are your friends? What did you not do?* Of course, bubbling underneath was the hardest questions we all crave answers to when we're faced with a crisis: *Why?* and *Why me?*

Recovery was slower than I hoped. A month after my treatment, I had barely enough energy to show up at Pioneer Memorial Church for Thursday Chapel and watch Alex Bryan speak for the Week of Prayer at Andrews University. This turned out to be one in a series of miracles that changed my life. I heard the voice of Jesus through Alex.

Alex and I connected and formed an instant friendship, talking about all kinds of things related to faith. Nine months later, after several of these conversations, we called five friends to join us for a two-day "retreat" in room 602 of the Holiday Inn in Denver, Colorado. Tim Gillespie, Sam Leonor, and Terry Swenson all flew in. Dany Hernandez (in Florida) and Eddie Hypolite (in London) joined us by

For the One

Skype and phone, as their respective time zones permitted.

We read the Bible together. We read the same books. We prayed. We fasted. We met for fellowship and honest conversation about the issues that mattered most to us—primarily our profound need for *more*.

I honestly can't remember the exact moment that the significance of our conversations sank in for all of us. Maybe it was when Terry asked us to share the stories that had brought us together. Maybe it was when Alex lifted us in song with "Jesus Loves Me This I Know." Perhaps when we laughed or cried like little children, when the red-lettered words of Jesus leapt out of the Bible like live embers into our dry wooden hearts and ignited once again the relentless passion for Jesus. But everything came together when Tim stopped the rapid-fire conversation suddenly and said, "Jesus (period) All (period)."

Jesus. All.

We realized in that moment—as Gabe Lyons in his book, *The Next Christians*, challenges readers—that we must, "recover the Gospel, . . . re-learn and fall in love again with that historic, beautiful, redemptive, faithful, demanding, reconciling, all-powerful, restorative, atoning, grace-abounding, soul-quenching, spiritually fulfilling good news of God's love,"[1] as expressed in Jesus.

Herein is the clincher for me: The Father sends us the Holy Spirit (see John 14). The Holy Spirit points us to Jesus (see John 15). And Jesus points us to the Father (see John 14). Do you see that endless circle in the Trinity? Father lifts up the Holy Spirit, Holy Spirit lifts up Jesus, Jesus lifts up the Father, Father to Holy Spirit, Holy Spirit to Jesus, Jesus to Father. When we see Jesus, it is because of the Holy Spirit. Then, by seeing Jesus we actually see the Father.

Jesus. All.

Jesus is in the whole Bible—Old and New Testaments. Every story teaches us about the nature of Jesus through His love and mercy. Even the genealogies teach us about the progression of humanity and the intervention of Jesus in our future.

Introduction

My personal theology for The One Project, for my local church community "One Place," and for my life, is embedded in the stories of Jesus found in Luke 15: everyone matters! But the breadth and depth of this truth are found in the entirety of Scripture. Hope, joy community—all in Jesus. They lead to the beauty that we are not alone.

I believe we all wish to hear the voice of Jesus in our lives. I cannot tell you enough how I know that is possible, real, palpable and tangible for all. That it is seen when you fall in love with Jesus because there is no other name that saves (see Acts 4).

Jesus. All.

It was with this re-kindled love for Jesus, this all-consuming reliance on Jesus, this indescribable quest to know more of Jesus, that we set up The One Project. Our mantra is "Jesus. All." and our mission is to "celebrate the supremacy of Jesus within the Seventh-day Adventist Church." We vowed to meet at least once a year for a "gathering." It would not be a summit, a conference, a symposium or a retreat. Rather, focusing on our experience in Denver, we felt we had found a void in our journey and the "gathering" would provide the much-needed space for us to hear the voice of Jesus.

These gatherings have grown and developed to include three essential elements:

1. Reflection: Our messages—such as those collected in this book—are limited to 18 minutes to articulate one stimulating reflection on Jesus.
2. Response: A live opportunity to question and engage for extra clarity with the Reflection.
3. Recalibrate: Most of our time is spent in dialogue with each other. It is here that we wrestle with application for ourselves, as well as for our local and global community. It is here that we have the hard, honest conversations about our heritage, legacy and trajectory.

These three elements mingled with physical and mental space help us to embrace "Jesus. All." Jesus still talks to us today.

I honestly, believe that the desire for these gatherings all over the world is—as Tim Gillespie shared with me once—"a sacred echo" that

For the One

has been heard. We are all inextricably linked together in Jesus. We might have once believed that we were like Elijah, all alone, until Jesus reminded us that He has "thousands" more of us out there. Our joy is to "gather" together and build networks that make a difference.

What follows in these pages are the first messages from men and women who honestly, want nothing more than to lift up Jesus.

Jesus. All.

---

1. Gabe Lyons (2010), *The Next Christians: The Good News About the End of Christian America*, Doubleday Books, page 192.

For the One

Introducing this book

Nathan Brown

"The One Project changed my life," she said bluntly. "I was thinking the church thing just wasn't for me but that was turned around and now I am involved again, with new enthusiasm and focus."

We were sharing a meal in a restaurant on the other side of the country, two friends of mine from different cities who had only just met each other—but had quickly found something, Some One, in common.

The second friend had a similar story. "A group of us from my church went to The One Project last year and came home wanting to share this with our church community," she said. "This has re-oriented our whole church. The young people who were part of our group have stepped up into leadership roles and the older people have been so supportive, as well as appreciating what we have added to our church life."

When people ask me what The One Project is about, I used to try to give a brief overview of the history, theology and format of The One Project gatherings. If you ask me that question today, I would introduce you to my friends Lidia and Lesleigh—or, at least, tell you a little of their stories. I could also tell you stories of other friends and the initiatives they have taken in response to the call to make Jesus all, to celebrate His supremacy in the Adventist church and to serve Him in their communities.

Similar stories were my first connection to The One Project. In mid-2011, a number of friends who had been part of the first gathering in Atlanta urged me to connect with The One Project as a new and

For the One

important thing happening within the church. What I found was a song that resonated in my heart and mind, calling our church to re-focus on the Jesus to whom the church and our lives rightly belong.

The One Project is one of the best and most important conversations happening in the Adventist church today. Because it is about Jesus. Because it draws on the best of our Adventist history and heritage. Because it grows out of a passion for our church, its progress and its vitality. Because it models a kind of conversation that moves beyond polarization and politicking. Because it is prompting people to serve others in real and practical ways. Because it is making a difference in the life of our church and the lives of many of my friends.

And these are all good reasons for this book, collecting some key pieces of this conversation over the past three years. But the pre-eminent reason and motivation must always be Jesus Himself.

Jesus . . .

> Familiar Friend but always and surprisingly unfamiliar.
>
> Son of God who preferred to describe Himself as Son of Man.
>
> Suffering Servant, crucified Criminal and kingdom's King.
>
> An actual, verifiable historical figure who calls us to His certain future.
>
> An ancient myth—in resurrected reality, alive and true today.
>
> His name a swear word that "will be the hope of all the world" (Matthew 12:21, NLT).
>
> Founder of a movement He would barely recognize, likely criticize, but love nonetheless.
>
> Ever-present "God with us," but so often achingly, disappointingly absent.
>
> Blessed hope that transforms today.
>
> Beginning with Matthew, Mark, Luke and John, subject of countless books, with this another—important, inadequate and incomplete though it be.

Jesus. All. But by no means is this all of Jesus.

Introduction

For some readers, this book might read like a "Greatest Hits" album from your favourite musicians. For others, this might be your first introduction to The One Project conversations. Wherever you are with this, we hope this book encourages you to connect and re-connect with Jesus, shining in and through, on and sometimes despite the context of Seventh-day Adventist faith.

As a collection of edited sermons given at different times by a number of presenters in various places, there are some inevitable overlaps and gaps, differences of perspective, style and tone, residual elements of spoken delivery, and a limited capacity to trace the growth of ideas over time. The selection of chapters has been made to represent the breadth of The One Project to this point in time, although some presentations are more easily adapted to a written format and this has influenced some selections.

Of course, the ideas and theology are important—that's why we've collected some of them in this book. "Jesus. All." is a profound theological statement and invites serious thought and engagement. But, as modelled at The One Project gatherings, this is best done in a community and in a context. One of the risks of collecting these presentations in book form is that we take them away from the context but we do so in hope of them finding other contexts and communities in which they can also speak—and in which Jesus can speak through them.

Of course, when a friend tells me The One Project has changed her life, I know she really means that Jesus changed her life. But The One Project helped her and Jesus to re-connect. As Jesus said, "If I am lifted up . . ." (see John 12:32).

When a friend tells me about the difference The One Project has made in her local church, I know that together they have re-focussed on Jesus. After all, Jesus said, "Where two or three are gathered in my name, there am I among them" (Matthew 18:20). And with Jesus among them, things will be different.

In similar ways, may this book help you and Jesus spend some time together and—working together—may you and He change your life, your church and your world.

For the One.

Jesus in Our History

Jesus

Our identity, our mission and our song

Tim Gillespie

I don't know what you have been called in your time in ministry or your involvement in church life. But let me tell you some of the labels I've been given at different times: a progressive Adventist, an emerging Adventist, an emergent Adventist, a historic Adventist, a missional Adventist, a conservative Adventist, a heretic, a social justice Adventist, an evangelical Adventist, a secular Adventist, a cultural Adventist, a true Adventist, an apostatized Adventist, a Christian Adventist, an Adventist Christian, a coffee drinker, lost, found, saved, saint, sinner, forgiven, a traditionalist, a non-traditionalist, a foundationalist, a non-foundationalist, a fundamentalist, liberal, compromiser, a creeping compromiser—and sometimes just "creep."

I've been accused of being a Jesuit. I am not a Jesuit. I'm not even sure how one would become a Jesuit. It seems like a lot of work. It isn't one of my hobbies.

I've been accused of being too academic, too silly, too funny, too boring, too fake, too authentic, too shallow, too deep, too theological, and not theological enough. I have been threatened with censure and even prayer. We've all had those conversations when someone says, "I'm going to pray for you." I never know how to respond. Perhaps "Well, I'm going to pray for *you*, too."

And I suppose at some time or another, the majority of these things have been true of me, even if only in a passing thought—except I'm not a Jesuit.

A new identity

Such labels have become part of our experience in church. Our church expresses its fears with political and faction-based rhetoric. These labels become a mark of identity. Are you progressive, liberal, conservative or historic?

Unfortunately, these marks place an identity that somehow—at least in our limited and intertwining circles—supersedes the identity that Christ has given us. Jürgen Moltmann says this about Christian identity: "Christian identity can be understood only as an act of identification with the crucified Christ, to the extent to which one has accepted the proclamation that in Him God has identified Himself with the godless and those abandoned by God, to whom one belongs oneself."[1] When you pick an identity beyond yourself, there is always movement in the life of faith.

So, what if we refused the labels? What if there was a group of people within this church that decided people couldn't call them anything because their identity was found in one thing: Jesus? Would this be the point where our interpretation of the Fundamental Beliefs became our expression of faith, rather than the mark and measure of our faithfulness? The supremacy of Christ should be our mark and measure of faith. But at what place do we put Jesus? I don't ask this question lightly. When you encounter Jesus, He becomes a priority. However, when you abide in Jesus, He becomes your elemental impulse.

Luke 6:45 tells us that your mouth speaks from the overflow of your heart. Is the overflow of your heart Jesus or have you spent the majority of your time talking about the church and its ecclesiology? Do you talk about your frustrations with the church, where it's heading and where you want it to go? That's what I've spent much of my time talking about. I have found myself fretting and worrying about my faith tradition. At first, I believe I was worried about my faith. However, it was my faith tradition that I was concerned for. I have found time and time again that the discussions on my lips have been about policy and quality of the church. My ecclesiology and what I thought of the church had greatly overshadowed my Christology. In the end, it was messing with my missiology.

The order of these things is important. My Christology had to come

Jesus in Our History

first: Who is Jesus? And who is Jesus to me? While I thought I had settled this question a long time ago, it seemed that it needed revisiting. It was time to re-establish the supremacy of Jesus Christ in my life.

I was drawn to the book of Colossians and Paul's clear thinking on the issue:

> The Son is the image of the invisible God, the firstborn over all creation. For in him all things were created: things in heaven and on earth, visible and invisible, whether thrones or powers or rulers or authorities; all things have been created through him and for him. He is before all things, and in him all things hold together. And he is the head of the body, the church; he is the beginning and the firstborn from among the dead, so that in everything he might have the supremacy. For God was pleased to have all his fullness dwell in him, and through him to reconcile to himself all things, whether things on earth or things in heaven, by making peace through his blood, shed on the cross. Once you were alienated from God and were enemies in your minds because of your evil behavior. But now he has reconciled you by Christ's physical body through death to present you holy in his sight, without blemish and free from accusation—if you continue in your faith, established and firm, and do not move from the hope held out in the gospel. This is the gospel that you heard and that has been proclaimed to every creature under heaven, and of which I, Paul, have become a servant (Colossians 1:15–23, NIV).

> It was time to re-establish the supremacy of Jesus Christ in my life.

What a stunningly elegant vision of Christ. He is exalted, glorious and lifted up. Paul used this revelation of how Christ is in hope that the Colossians would find their way back to the One. Paul bet that Christ would heal them and show them the way. He was the only thing that could bind them together. Christ is the image of the invisible God—and God was content to put the fullness of Himself right into Jesus.

For the One

Paul went on to say that the thing that holds the universe together, let alone my faith tradition, is Jesus. Without Christ, my universe, my faith and my church fall apart.

In Colossians, we find that the Judaizers—another identity tag—had caused problems for the church. The church was primarily made up of Christians from gentile backgrounds. Some were saying that Jesus wasn't enough. The old law was just a shadow. In Ephesus, we find Paul saying the same thing, giving Timothy warnings about people who add emphasis to endless genealogy. It was also a problem on the island of Crete. In the region of Galatia, men came from Jerusalem and even persuaded Peter for a time to look somewhere else.

Re-discovering Christology

In this journey, I began to understand the blessing that I have in holding my faith tradition high when it comes to Jesus because a high Christology is the elemental impulse of the pioneers of the Seventh-day Adventist Church. But I'm trying to explain Jesus in the church today. Ultimately, this is a question of Christology in its rightful place within the Seventh-day Adventist context. As we see today, does that Christology influence our missiology? And does that Christology inform our ecclesiology as well?

In Frost and Hirsch's book *The Shaping of Things to Come*, they make a case that our Christology informs our missiology, which determines our ecclesiology.[2] This is imperative for our understanding of today's church. It seems that perhaps our Christology is assumed: "You've got Jesus? Good, I'd like to talk about some weightier things now." On one occasion, I had somebody come up to me and tell me that I talk about Jesus a lot. They asked me when I was going to move on. Well, I'm not. They asked me when I was going to talk about the heavy theological things. I said, "Oh, you mean those heavy theological things that only gain weight when they are embodied by Jesus Christ? Are those the things you are talking about?"

Our missiology has always been clearly defined for us and our ecclesiology has been inherited, healthy or not. I think that has led us to become wrapped up in discussions about the church. We talk about the church. We label those in church as "good" or "bad." We spend time

Jesus in Our History

wondering if we are really doing God's work as defined by the church. We see our Christ through the lens of the church, rather than seeing our church through the lens of Jesus Christ.

Let me be clear: I don't deny the power of the fellowship of believers. However, just as our identity is found in Christ alone, so must our mission be identified by who we believe Christ to be. And our fellowship and church is identified with its connection to Christ and how it expresses that connection in the world.

To have the church define Christ is dangerous. The bride did not ask the groom for the relationship, it was the groom who asked. The church is the bride of Christ only because He asked us to be, not because we have any place or title from which to attract Him. We are misbehaved, ungrateful, ungracious and unflatteringly ugly. Yet in our proper place underneath His supremacy, we are loved and even sacrificed for. The Bridegroom has deemed us worthy of relationship.

But rather than spending time doting on the Bridegroom, we are spending our time concerned about the wedding dress. We are in danger of becoming obsessed with looking at ourselves in the mirror. And when narcissism leads to excluding those we deem unworthy of the grace of God, we are in danger of telling the Bridegroom whom He can and cannot love. That is not our place. Christology—missiology—ecclesiology: this is the order that assumes a high place for Jesus in our experience and in our church.

> Just as our identity is found in Christ alone, so must our mission be identified by who we believe Christ to be.

Re-discovering present truth

How many of us know people who feel they have left the church to maintain their connection with Christ? This is a sobering question and the statistics on this are staggering in North America. While there are certainly developmental issues within churches that send people away, the term "cultural Adventist" is not foreign to us. You can grow up in this church and not know Jesus. I graduated with 55 people

For the One

from a Seventh-day Adventist high school; today, only three of us claim Adventism.

And I want to declare my appreciation for my church-tribe, because this is the place I met Jesus. I met Him through a strong grace-centered upbringing. I was surrounded by such wonderful Christians, theologians, teachers, pastors and people who understood the supremacy of Christ. So many people in our church do and there's a hum that comes with a high Christology.

However, I fear that our faith has become defensive. As it becomes defensive, it begins to choke down its own songs. Moltmann once again says,

> Faith is fearful and defensive when it begins to die inwardly, struggling to maintain itself and reaching out for security and guarantees. In so doing, it removes itself from the hand of the One who has promised to maintain it. And its own manipulations bring it to ruin. The pugilistic faith usually occurs in the form of an orthodoxy that feels threatened and is therefore more rigid than ever.[3]

Before the group of us met in Denver, I was questioning my place within the Seventh-day Adventist Church. But we have a rich history of being open. The preamble of our statement of beliefs gives us hope:

> Seventh-day Adventists accept the Bible as their only creed and hold certain fundamental beliefs to be the teachings of the Holy Scriptures. These beliefs, as set forth here, constitute the church's understanding and expression of the teachings of scripture. Revision of these statements may be expected at a General Conference session when the church is led by the Holy Spirit to a fuller understanding of Bible truth or finds better language to express the teachings of God's Holy Word.[4]

We are open to change. We are open to a reorientation. The only reason we can say this in the preamble is because it aligns with the words Ellen White says in her take on "present truth":

> There is no excuse for anyone in taking the position that there is no more truth to be revealed, and that all our expositions of Scripture are without an error. The fact that

certain doctrines have been held as truth for many years by our people, is not a proof that our ideas are infallible. Age will not make error into truth, and truth can afford to be fair. No true doctrine will lose anything by close investigation. . . . As real spiritual life declines, it has ever been the tendency to cease to advance in the knowledge of the truth. Men rest satisfied with the light already received from God's word, and discourage any further investigation of the Scriptures. They become conservative, and seek to avoid discussion.[5]

These quotes give me hope. They let me see that from early in our history, Adventists have dealt with some of the same issues we do today. But honestly, sometimes I feel out of place.

On one occasion, I was on a panel in a discussion at Loma Linda, and it seemed to be set up with the very conservative on the right and then gradually more liberal. I was late so they ended up sitting me on the very left.

The moderator kept referring to what the conservatives wanted to discuss as "the settled truth." Finally, I said, "Excuse me, but I have no idea what you mean by 'settled truth.'"

And he just looked at me as if to say, "You don't get it? Like, it's the word *settled*. It's done."

So I said, "Yeah, that's not Adventist. Actually, that's the most un-Adventist phrase I've ever heard."

And I loved it because everyone on the other side of the table agreed with me. It was interesting because during the discussion, each side wanted to talk about their agenda, but I just wanted to engage the discussion about Jesus. I thought everyone could agree on that.

I wanted to talk about Jesus because I didn't want to fight. I wanted to lift Him up. That's my calling. My job is not to be right; it is to be in Christ. My job is to explore the wonders of His mercy and His grace together, in community.

We will live different lifestyles. We will prioritize different things because we are different people, built differently from the DNA up. But

> From early in our history, Adventists have dealt with some of the same issues we do today.

we have this tie that binds us and His name is Jesus. You can't argue about the truth of Jesus, you can only argue about the truth of how we speak of Jesus. However, Jesus supersedes even how we explain Him. Jesus transcends our foolish and awkward words and is this beautiful mystery we can all enjoy—and all be challenged by.

Another song

For me, our initial meeting in Denver was an incarnation of the hope that I am not alone in this. And The One Project is an incarnation of this same hope on a much broader scale. In Denver, it was just a small group of us humming this resonant tone.

It seemed to me at the time that I was being left out of all the songs being sung from all the hills in our Seventh-day Adventist context—be those mountains or molehills. The songs of the "right" were too rigid and fearful for my taste, with little opportunity to improvise or be playful. The songs on the "left" were at times incoherent and melody-less. How I longed for the song that would be the very resonant tone of my heart. I longed for it to burst forward, out of me because of its very nature. I was listening.

As a songwriter, you realize that there are songs deep within you. There are songs that you don't so much write, but they write themselves. The gentleman who made my guitar used to say, "You know, that guitar has a lot of songs in it." That was just another way of saying that it has a tone that could stir something deep within.

In my church conversations and interactions, there was this longing and desire for a song that made sense to me. I longed for a melody that somehow both included and transcended the folk tunes of our faith, those peculiar melodies that cradled me as my faith matured, but ultimately left me longing for more. Where was the common line or the resonating tone that would bring this cacophony together?

I was not expecting the type of melody that would make everyone lockstep into formation. Instead, I'm interested in a dynamic unity. I'm interested in people with different beliefs and worldviews going toward the same goal and knowing we need each other. It's like when you hear an orchestra as they begin to tune up. You hear the noise begin to grow. It's not really music, more of a welling of this feeling that something is

Jesus in Our History

about to happen. There's a feeling that there are people from different places, with different instruments, beginning to prepare.

I love when the violins begin to tune because the sound rises above everything. Then it's silent for a moment—and you know it's about to happen. You know that this multitude of musicians with different instruments are all going to come under the headship of the conductor. He is about to give them the song that will bring them together.

And the music that's made brings tears to your eyes. You are so moved by people who aren't conformed to the same thing but, in unity, are going about the parts that they have been given specifically. It is a beautiful and joyful noise. It is a tie that binds.

It is the same with a community of faith coming together and acknowledging that Jesus Christ is alive. Jesus Christ is above all. Jesus Christ is the mark and measure of our faith.

And I will accept no identity tag other than that I am a Christian and believe in Jesus Christ. Call me what you will—but I love Jesus.

---

1. Jürgen Moltmann, *The Crucified God: The Cross of Christ as the Foundation and Criticism of Christianity,* Fortress Press, 1973, page 19.

2. Michael Frost and Alan Hirsch, *The Shaping of Things to Come: Innovation and Mission for the 21st-Century Church*, Hendrickson Publishers, 2003, page 209.

3. Moltmann, ibid.

4. "Preamble," 28 Fundamental Beliefs of the Seventh-day Adventist Church.

5. Ellen White, *Counsels to Writers and Editors*, pages 35, 38.

They Heard a Voice
Jesus in our story

Sam Leonor

The earliest record of Adventist history is in Genesis 1. The supremacy and authority of Jesus is evident even in the Creation story. He spoke, "Let there be light," and the result was immediate—there was light. The Creation story begins and ends with His voice. "Then God blessed them, and God said to them, 'Be fruitful and multiply; fill the earth'" (Genesis 1:28, NIV). We should always begin there.

Later, John described the coming of God to the world by saying, "The Word"—this same Word, through and by whom we were made—"became one of us" (see John 1:10) And then this Word, in His voice, began to call us—ordinary men and women. He said to them—and He says to us—"Come, follow Me."

He didn't—and doesn't—call people to follow a religion, a denomination, a congregation, a preacher, a cause or a movement. He calls them to Himself. Matthew 4:19–21 reads, "'Come, follow me,' Jesus said, 'and I will make you fishers of men.' . . . At once . . . ." It's like an instinctive reaction. It's like they knew, they recognized, they obeyed. They knew that Voice. "At once they left their nets and followed him."

Before they behaved right, before they believed right, they recognized a Voice and they knew—I will follow this Man. I will belong to Him. They left everything behind. All they had was Jesus. They didn't know where they were going, what they were being called to. They weren't sure who He was, but they were attracted to this Person. They recognized something in Him.

When he was called, Paul experienced something similar (see Acts 9): "Saul, Saul, why do you persecute me?"

Paul said, "Who are you?"

Jesus in Our History

"I am Jesus, whom you are persecuting."

And his transformation was so incredible that Paul later wrote to the Corinthians, "For I resolved to know nothing while I was with you except Jesus Christ and him crucified" (1 Corinthians 2:2, NIV).

Later, from prison, his body broken from years of beatings, stonings, lashings and more, Paul wrote to the Philippians as he was about to die, "And my God will meet all of your needs according to his glorious riches in Christ Jesus" (Philippians 4:19, NIV). In Jesus, we have all we need!

Some time ago, there was an exhibit of Jean-Léon Gérôme's work at The J Paul Getty Museum in Los Angeles. I took my kids and we were walking around looking at this art. Suddenly, we came around a corner and there it was, "The Christian Martyr's Last Prayer." I fell apart at the Getty, weeping. It's so painful. I looked into the faces of the people, the Christians who are about to die, and there's a girl about my daughter's age. I kept thinking, *What were they hearing at that moment? What could they see?* I believe they heard a Voice, and the Voice was the voice of Jesus saying, "You have all you need. You have Me."

The Reformers heard a Voice. So many of them were burned at the stake and died horrible deaths. One example is Jan Hus (also known as John Huss) who led the Reformation movement in what is now the Czech Republic, where the Reformation actually failed. During his trial, Jan was about to be burned at the stake and was offered a way out: "Do it our way and you get to live."

Ellen White wrote of his death, "When the body of Huss had been wholly consumed, his ashes, with the soil upon which they rested, were gathered up and cast into the Rhine, and thus borne onward to the ocean, his persecutors vainly imagined that they had rooted out the truths he preached. Little did they dream that the ashes that day borne away to the sea were to be as seed scattered in all the countries of the earth; that in lands yet unknown it would yield abundant fruit in witnesses for the truth."[1] You cannot hide or bury the truth!

William Miller heard a Voice, he recognized the Voice and he followed it. While studying the Bible, he concluded, "I had to admit that the

For the One

scriptures must be a revelation from God. They became my delight and in Jesus I found a Friend." Of Jesus, he said, "God opened my eyes and what a Savior I discovered Jesus to be. My sins fell from my soul. The Bible spoke of Jesus. He was on every page."

So Miller gathered his followers on October 22, 1844. And on that day we did not have the Sabbath. We did not have a correct understanding of the trinity or the state of the dead. We didn't have rules about pork, coffee, gluten, soy, cheese, chicken, or beef. We didn't have "Blue Zones." We didn't have conferences or unions or divisions or the General Conference. Before Ellen White had her first vision, we were about one thing. We had an all-consuming, irrepressible, irresistible, overpowering, radical desire to be with Jesus.

"Although I have been twice disappointed, I am not yet cast down or discouraged," Miller wrote. "I have fixed my mind upon another time and here I mean to stand until God gives me more light; and that is today, today, today until He comes and I see Him for whom my soul yearns." He did not speak about streets of gold, friendly lions, mansions and crowns; His soul yearned for Jesus—for the One.

What does our soul yearn for? As a people, as Adventists, what do we yearn for?

We can argue all we want about 1888, but I think two guys, Ellet Waggoner and Alonzo Jones, heard a Voice and they were right about one thing. They were right about Jesus. Ellen White called their message "a most precious message. A message that was to bring more prominently before the world the uplifted Savior—the sacrifice for the sins of the whole world. It presented justification through faith in surety and invited the people to receive the righteousness of Christ."

Ellen White also heard the Voice! She'd been hearing it, but here things got serious for her and she recognized it. She began to point out that the church was more focused on itself than on Jesus. For that and other reasons, she was sent to Australia to "encourage the work." She was already in her 60s, and the average life expectancy for a woman in the 1890s was mid-60s. In effect, they exiled her. She was ill. She had a hard time adjusting to the culture. She was homesick.

Then William Warren Prescott visited her. Prescott showed up at a camp meeting in Melbourne and something happened to her while he preached. He explained that a change had come to him like a personal revelation. He no longer believed that the thing to do was to prove the doctrines, to simply demonstrate their truthfulness. Doctrines needed to be presented as the gospel rightly understood. They should grow out of a belief in Jesus Christ as the living Savior. Adventists, he believed, needed a total re-orientation of their belief structure. Christ must be the center of everything.

This sermon series so affected Ellen that, with Marian Davis at her side, she began to compile work she had been putting together from the 1850s, sensing it was time for *The Desire of Ages*.

In 1895, the General Conference was practically begging her to come back. She said, "No." The main reason given was that she had financial difficulties. But I think it's because she now had all she needed. She had Jesus. It took Stephen Haskell to convince her to travel home to help with some pressing issues.

The Desire of Ages book had a pivotal effect on us. For one thing, this line, "For in Christ there is life eternal, unborrowed,"[2] finally settled the Arianist question. It influenced leaders like Carlyle Haynes to preach sermons that called us back to Jesus. At the 1926 General Conference session, he said, "The inmost central glory of the gospel therefore is not a great truth nor a great message nor a great movement, but a great Person. It is Jesus Christ Himself. Without Him there could be no gospel. He came, not so much as to declare a message, but rather that there might be a message to proclaim. He Himself was and is the message, not His teachings, but He Himself constituted Christianity."

Blanca Pol is 104 years old. She loves Jesus so much. She didn't finish high school. She never read Barth, Moltmann, Schaeffer or Lucado for that matter. But she loves Jesus so much and she heard His Voice— and in 1934, she went to Antonio and Josefa Rivera's house. Antonio was a

For the One

poor carpenter and, while listening to Blanca, he and his wife heard the Voice, too, and they followed. They were my grandparents.

In 1972, my parents went to Nicaragua to work in developing healthcare missions. In the 1990s when I learned some things about Latin American history, wars and revolution—I told my father, "You were nuts! In 1972, Central America was in the middle of a civil war. There were people dying on our campus. There were bullets flying around. Why did you move our family there? What were you thinking?"

And he simply says, every time I ask him this question, "We were called there and we obeyed." They heard a Voice—and they had to respond.

Me, I was playing the part of Jesus during a passion play at Nosoca Pines Ranch summer camp one day. Hanging on a cross made from cheap planks, wearing ketchup to look like blood, fire ants crawling all over me, the cross leaning over, I heard a Voice. It's hard to explain what it felt like. Chris Blake comes close to explaining the feeling in his book, *Searching for a God to Love*. He says it so beautifully and it's actually how I felt: "Our love affair with God isn't an arranged marriage to a demanding partner, a fate worse than death. It's more like a spirited adventure, like otters in the ocean swimming in the assurance of deep, safe love."[3]

Do you hear it? Jesus calls us. He calls us. He calls our church. You can't bury this Voice. It will continue to call.

A couple of years ago, a student was brought to me. She was in a wheelchair because she contracted something that began to deteriorate her nervous system. She couldn't walk, and during a period of two years she had lost her sight almost completely. They brought her into my office, and she just wanted to talk about what her future was going to be like. For four or five months, every week, we talked and prayed together. We prayed for healing and eventually, I began to say to her, "Do you have Jesus? If you have Jesus, Paul says, that's all you need."

At the end of the school year, she came by my office and dropped off a card written in Braille. She had my secretary write a sticky note that read, "I have all I need. I have Jesus." The Braille read, "We walk by

Jesus in Our History

faith, not by sight."

In September, when school began again, my office was loud. I was talking to somebody, then suddenly, the room fell quiet. You could sense someone looking. Everyone turned to the doorway where a girl was weeping. She pointed at me and said, "You are Pastor Sam. I've known your voice. I can see you!"

During the summer, her medical team figured out her problem and began treatment that eventually cured her. She could see now!

I believe there is a day coming when we will all stand in the Presence. We will hear the Voice that brought it all into existence at Creation, the Voice that called the first disciples, the reformers and our Adventist pioneers. We will hear the Voice that calls us today and has always called us to Himself, and we will say, "It's you! I have known your Voice. I can see you now!"

1. Ellen White, *The Great Controversy,* page 110.

2. Ellen White, *The Desire of Ages*, page 530.

3. Chris Blake, *Searching for a God to Love*, Pacific Press. 1999, pages 246–7.

> We will hear the voice that calls us today and has always called us to Himself.

Primal Adventism

Jesus at our beginning

Alex Bryan

The stream of Adventism is fed by the teardrops of the Great Disappointment.

We can't understand the currents of this movement, the flow of its theology, the rapids of its hopes and hang-ups, what floats it and at times drowns it, its eschatological energy, the life of its lifestyle, nor the refreshing river of its anthropological vision without an empathetic grasp of the October 22, 1844, punch in the gut.

It didn't happen on that day. He didn't appear. The clock struck midnight, and the Adventists were wrong. Tragically wrong. A whopper of a theological mistake. We argued from the Bible that the second coming of Jesus would happen on this date. We quit our jobs, left our homes, walked out of our churches. We sold our stuff. We looked to the sky. But there was no trumpet. There were no angels. There was no cloud.

The Advent movement was born in failure rather than success, error rather than truth, darkness rather than light, and sorrow rather than joy.

Jesus didn't return.

The Great Disappointment.

Here is a truth: disappointments clarify, purging the streams of our lives of substances that might have clouded them. The disappointments of our lives bring sharper vision. They enable us to see who we are and what we are about. They make the hearts of men and women transparent.

In the fall of 1996, the Atlanta Braves—whom I adore—led the New

Jesus in Our History

York Yankees—whom I abhor—two games to one in the baseball World Series. At one point in game four, they held a six-run lead, and in the eighth innings they were still three runs ahead when Mark Wohlers, one of the Braves' better pitchers, threw a hanging slider—a very bad pitch. Jim Leyritz, the Yankee catcher, connected with that pitch, hitting a game-tying three-run homer over the left-field wall. The Yankees won that game in extra innings, and they went on to win the World Series.

I'll bet you couldn't care less about the Braves' loss. It was 15 years ago, and you might not even have lost two seconds of sleep that very night. Well, *I* did. I was so disappointed that I tossed, turned and fidgeted, replaying that home run over and over again in my mind. And for days afterward, I talked with friends about the game: "Did you see what happened? Can you believe it?"

And now, a decade and a half later, I'm writing about it. In detail!

What does this reveal about me? That I've got some serious sports addiction issues? Whether healthy or not, this disappointment is clarifying. It says that Alex Bryan loves baseball and the Atlanta Braves baseball team. It reveals me.

When she breaks up with you and you cry and you listen to sad songs on the radio and you write sappy poetry and you mope and you can't seem to cope, your disappointment reveals that you care deeply for *her*.

When you break up with her and 10 minutes later she is shopping and fielding calls from other guys, happy and free, her lack of disappointment reveals what—or who—she *doesn't* care about. (Hint: *You*.)

When a son looks for his father in the stands, a father who fails to show up for his son's basketball game, the look of disappointment speaks.

When a daughter looks for her mother in the audience, a mother who fails to show up for her daughter's violin concert, the look of disappointment speaks.

These looks say, "I care about my girlfriend's/boyfriend's/parent's approval, love, affection, participation, presence in my life. I'm disappointed when they're absent because *I care about them and what they think about me*."

One day I'll find the emotional courage to tell the full story of Nicole's and my years-long struggle with infertility. We couldn't have children.

For the One

We spent big money on cutting-edge medical experimentation, but our baby dreams rested on techniques that just wouldn't work. I'll never forget hearing a good scientist with horrible bedside manner tell my wife and me in a surgical recovery room, "I'm sorry. There's nothing there, and there never will be. You won't have children. You need to move on." The look on my wife's face: crushing disappointment. And I'm sure the look on my face revealed that my heart was shredded too.

We were humans who desperately wanted to become parents. It was our sorrow that pulled back the curtain that covered the deepest places of the soul. Pain made our desire clear.[1]

The Great Disappointment

When things don't disappoint us, we know that we don't care about them. When things disappoint us a little bit, we know that we care a little bit. But when we feel *great disappointment*, we know whatever caused it matters an awful lot.

Adventism was distilled by the Great Disappointment of October 22, 1844. How Adventists reacted to what didn't happen on that day clarifies the content of this Christian faith stream. Here's what some Adventists who experienced October 22 said about what it meant to them:

> *Henry Emmons:* "I waited all Tuesday and *dear Jesus* did not come. I waited all forenoon of Wednesday, and was well in body as I ever was, but after 12 o'clock I began to feel faint, and before dark I needed someone to help me up to my chamber, as my natural strength was leaving me fast, and I lay prostrate for two days without pain—sick with disappointment."[2]

> *Washington Morse:* "That day came and passed, and the darkness of another night closed in upon the world. But with that darkness came a pang of disappointment to the Advent believers that can find a parallel only in the sorrow of the disciples after the crucifixion of *their Lord*. The passing of time was a bitter disappointment. True believers had given

Jesus in Our History

up *all for Christ*, and had shared His presence as never before. *The love of Jesus filled every soul; and with inexpressible desire they prayed, 'Come, Lord Jesus, and come quickly;' but He did not come.*"[3]

Hiram Edson: "Our fondest hopes and expectations were blasted, and such a spirit of weeping came over us as I never experienced before. It seemed that *the loss of all earthly friends* could have been no comparison. We wept, and wept, till the day dawn."[4]

Seventeen-year-old Ellen White: "Those who *sincerely love Jesus* can appreciate the feelings of those who watched with the most *intense longing* for the coming of their Savior."[5]

> **Christianity was conceived in response to the life, death and resurrection of Jesus of Nazareth.**

All religious movements have a beginning. They have a foundational, formational, inaugural, initial reason for existence.
- Judaism was born as an organized religion when Moses heard God's voice atop Mount Sinai.
- Islam sprang from the belief that Allah revealed insights to the Prophet Muhammad, who lived about 1400 years ago. The Koran contains these revelations.
- Christianity was conceived in response to the life, death and resurrection of Jesus of Nazareth. A group of men and women believed what He said about Himself and about them. They believed He rose from the dead, so they believed *Him*.

For 2000 years, all sorts of Christian sects, movements, denominations, organizations and reorganizations have come to be:
- Because of theological and political differences, Christianity split

into Eastern and Western churches in the Great Schism of 1054.
- The Church of England was founded in 1534, when, due to a personal and political rift, King Henry VIII declared himself head of the church in place of the pope.
- The desire to reform the Roman Catholic Church eventually gave birth to Lutheranism and other Protestant traditions.
- Methodism was launched because of the piety of Charles and John Wesley.
- Convictions about liturgy—Was baptism for children or adults? Was *this* music or *that* music acceptable? Should the worship experience favor emotionalism or an emotion-free experience?—were behind the founding of some movements.
- Some groups were born out of a disagreement over a social issue, such as the role of women or homosexuals in the church.
- Some began in opposition to, or support of, some doctrinal issue.
- Some began opposing or supporting violence or war.
- Some began because of the teaching of some particular theologian.
- Many began because a man or woman claimed to have had special or secret encounters with an angel or with God Himself.

Adventism wasn't born as a reform movement, though it soon adopted various reforms. Adventism wasn't born as a temperance movement, though it found something to say about healthful living. Adventism wasn't born as a theological movement, as a correction of already existing denominations, nor in response to some liturgical or lifestyle concern. And despite its prophet, Adventism didn't come into being because of unique, private prophetic revelations. Adventism was born because of a wrong calculation about the Second Coming . . . fuelled by an intense, emotional, highly personal, fervent, and *ultimately right* desire to be with Jesus.

Adventism—*primal Adventism*—was about men and women who longed to be with Jesus.

The Desire of the Ages

The stream of Adventism is fed by the teardrops of the Great Disappointment. The cries of pain at its birth reveal intense affection

Jesus in Our History

and love for Jesus and an unsurpassed longing to be with Him. This is Adventism distilled. This is Adventism made most clear.

What makes Adventists unique? How would you answer this question?

I'd answer it by pointing to our unique beginning. Adventism isn't peculiar or special because of our Sabbath-keeping, vegetarian cuisine, or remnant claims. Adventism's uniqueness is found at its historical root: Jesus.

Whatever else has been thrown into these Adventist waters over the past 170 years (much of it good, though perhaps some of it not so good), the river of this religion is all about loving Christ.

Adventism's nearly two-century-old hang-up is . . . Jesus.

I slid the back door open to let the dog out. Helium balloon in hand, Audrey, our four-year-old theologian, asked, "Daddy, if I let this go, would it go all the way up to Jesus?"

I paused to reflect on what answer I should give. (You have to be careful about these things.) "Yes," I said. "It would go all the way up to Jesus."

She pondered that lofty reality for a quiet moment or two. "Well, Daddy, when would He get it back to me?"

I had to think about that a little longer. "Soon," I said. "Soon."

> When we worship and love Him, and when His love moves us to serve and love others, Adventism shines.

Adventism *at its best* takes the balloons of life and somehow hears what they say about Jesus—the balloons of work and play, joy and sorrow, holiness, theology, doctrine, priorities, relationships, and even church. When we find Jesus in the middle of our lives, we are on the right track. When we worship and love Him, and when His love moves us to serve and love others, Adventism shines.

Jesus today. Jesus now.

But Adventism *at its best* also looks up. It searches the skies with the very same hope that the Adventists of October 22, 1844, had. To be with Jesus. To enter His embrace and find a world without suffering and pain; sans tears and disappointment.

For the One

Adventism—again, *at its best*—has eyes that look up . . . not with fear-mongering predictions about the end of the world, not with wild speculations about when it will happen and how. Instead, with eyes filled with hope, humility, and love.

Jesus, later today—and if not today, then tomorrow.

The One

Is Jesus worth the tears and the desire? This enduring and endearing passion?

John 3:16 says, "God so loved the world, that He gave His only begotten Son" (KJV).

"Only begotten"? The Word is actually *monogenes*.

Mono: unique, one, one of a kind. Monochrome: one color. Monotone: one pitch. Monopoly: the one who has it all.

The One.

The look. The sound. The One who has it all.

Genes: genetics, human genes, *Homo sapiens*, DNA.

A One-of-a-kind human being.

There have been, and there are, lots of human beings—billions and billions over many generations. But God did something special in this one case. God poured God—all of God—into a human zygote. A human egg from one of Mary's ovaries, fertilized by the Spirit. And nine months later He was born: the Superhuman.

The beginning of Adventist anthropology—the search for who we are as human beings, our meaning, our purpose, our existence, our gene pool—is in the *monogenes*, Jesus Christ. Not just any Jesus. Not just a word we use to fill in whatever secular scheme or religious regime we concoct. Jesus, the historical. Jesus, the real. The one-and-only Jesus. The Jesus of the Gospels. The One who holds certain values. Particular priorities. A very definite view of God, humanity, and the earth.

Jesus isn't a big deal. Jesus is *The Deal*.

1 John 5:12 makes this bold claim: "He that hath the Son hath life; and he that hath not the Son of God hath not life" (KJV). So we can say, the denomination that hath the Son hath life; and the denomination that hath not the Son of God hath not life.

Adventism was born nearly two centuries ago in "the global West."

But now in America, Europe and Australia, Adventism finds itself (along with many other branches of Christianity) facing great challenges.

But the future of Adventism doesn't rest in master plans and master prayers. The future of Adventism doesn't find its hope in church structure, finances, new ways of articulating truth, creative approaches to theology, new or old worship, old-fashioned or new-fashioned ideas, or a longing for tomorrow or for yesterday. The future of Adventism is neither top down or bottom up.

So what *is the future*? Here's my proposal: If Adventism is to have a bright, energetic, vibrant future . . . If Adventism is going to get a life and have a life . . . it must—we must—have the Son.

In 1842, during this era of Advent hope, 15-year-old Ellen White had a mystical experience. Her memoir points us to the heart of this movement. Listen to how Ellen White described her "Green Cord Dream":

> Soon after this I had another dream. I seemed to be sitting in abject despair, with my face in my hands, reflecting like this: If Jesus were upon earth, I would go to Him, throw myself at His feet, and tell Him all my sufferings. He would not turn away from me; He would have mercy upon me, and I would love and serve Him always.
>
> Just then the door opened, and a person of beautiful form and countenance entered. He looked upon me pitifully, and said: "Do you wish to see Jesus? He is here, and you can see Him if you desire it. Take everything you possess, and follow me."
>
> I heard this with unspeakable joy, and gladly gathered up my little possessions, every treasured trinket, and followed my guide. He led me to a steep and apparently frail stairway. As I began to ascend the steps, he cautioned me to keep my eyes fixed upward, lest I should grow dizzy and fall. Many

> If Adventism is to have a bright, energetic, vibrant future . . . If Adventism is going to get a life and have a life . . .

For the One

others who were climbing the steep ascent fell before gaining the top.

Finally we reached the last step, and stood before a door. Here my guide directed me to leave all the things that I had brought with me. I cheerfully laid them down. He then opened the door, and bade me enter. In a moment I stood before Jesus. There was no mistaking that beautiful countenance; that expression of benevolence and majesty could belong to no other. As His gaze rested upon me, I knew at once that He was acquainted with every circumstance of my life and all my inner thoughts and feelings.

I tried to shield myself from His gaze, feeling unable to endure His searching eyes; but He drew near with a smile, and laying His hand upon my head, said, "Fear not." The sound of His sweet voice thrilled my heart with a happiness it had never before experienced. I was too joyful to utter a word, but, overcome with emotion, sank prostrate at His feet. While I was lying helpless there, scenes of beauty and glory passed before me, and I seemed to have reached the safety and peace of heaven. At length my strength returned, and I arose. The living eyes of Jesus were still upon me, and His smile filled my soul with gladness. His presence awoke in me a holy reverence and an inexpressible love.

My guide now opened the door, and we both passed out. He bade me take up again all the things I had left without. This done, he handed me a green cord coiled up closely. This he directed me to place next to my heart, and when I wished to see Jesus, take it from my bosom, and stretch it to the utmost. He cautioned me not to let it remain coiled for any length of time, lest it should become knotted and difficult to straighten. I placed the cord near my heart, and joyfully descended the narrow stairs, praising the Lord, and telling all whom I met where they could find Jesus.[6]

This is the primal heart of Adventism. He is our Desire, our Lord, and our Friend.

1. Miracle of miracles, and miracle of miracles again, we now have two children, born without the aid of modern fertility science.

2. George Knight, *A Search for Identity: The Development of Seventh-day Adventist Beliefs,* Review and Herald Publishing Association, 2000, page 53, emphasis added.

3. George Knight, *A Brief History of Seventh-day Adventists* (Second Edition), Review and Herald, 2004, page 25, emphasis added.

4. ibid, emphasis added.

5. Ellen White, *Life Sketches of Ellen White,* Pacific Press Publishing Association, 1915, page 56, emphasis added.

6. ibid, pages 34–6.

The Forgotten Legacy of 1844

Jesus in our disappointment

Lisa Clark Diller

I grew up with a story. It was a true story, but one of those true stories that I heard so often that it began to seem timeless and mythological. It was a story of a man named William Miller.

While he was fighting in the War of 1812, Miller had an amazing conversion experience. Like many people, he took the fact that he had remained safe amid the dangers of the battlefield as a sign that God was with him. He decided there really was a *personal* God.

Further participation in the life of the Christian community exposed him to more intensive investigation into scripture. One day, according to his own words, while reading the Bible:

> The character of a Savior was vividly impressed upon my mind. It seemed that there might be a Being so good and compassionate as to Himself atone for our transgressions. . . . I immediately felt how lovely such a Being must be and imagined that I could cast myself into the arms of, and trust in the mercy of, such a One. . . . The Bible did bring to view just such a Savior as I needed. . . . The scriptures must [then] be a revelation from God. They became my delight and in Jesus I found a friend.[1]

Jesus in Our History

Scripture revealed something far more powerful than the personal God shared by monotheistic religions around the world. Miller found the God Incarnate and he believed that the Bible was true because it testified to the Word made flesh.

A way to study

But this isn't the part that I found really interesting as I was growing up. What was compelling to me about William Miller was the rationalism and the methodical way he went about studying the Scriptures. The story—as I always heard it (which is the way Miller himself told it)—was that he was so compelled by the rationality of Scripture and its reliability as a source of information that he decided to read through the Bible starting with Genesis 1:1 and would not move forward with the next verse until he understood the one he was reading.

This was really exciting to me as a young, budding nerd. For my Seventh-day Adventist upbringing, the point of this story was that when he got to Daniel, he started sorting out the prophecies there—especially the 2300-day prophecy—and arrived at the conclusion that Jesus would be coming back in 1843. When Jesus didn't come in 1843, there was a crisis, then a recalculation and a decision that 1844 was the better date. When Jesus didn't come on October 22, 1844, the crisis of faith and knowledge that followed was known as the Great Disappointment. One response to that disappointment was a Spirit-led reformulation of theology that spawned the Adventist church.

For a devout Seventh-day Adventist little girl in West Virginia who was afflicted with mostly untreated myopia and spent a great deal of time in corners staring at books, the example of someone who found "new truth" by reading the Bible carefully in order to solve its puzzles was a challenge that could not go unmet. Since by my teen years I'd read the Bible through many times and had mostly figured I understood everything (the simple confidence of youth is a beautiful thing), and since I was intellectually greedy enough to want some prophetic territory of my own, I decided to start with the prophetic book that mostly gets ignored. I decided to investigate Ezekiel.

I spent my entire freshman year of high school on Ezekiel. I was able to make fairly steady progress, sorting out the weird beings with animal-like attributes and angel messengers, until it came time to think about the extensive treatment given to the measurements and descriptions of the temple featured in the last eight chapters. I got really bogged down there. Someone with more visual imagination might still be able to make a thriving theological career out of Ezekiel. Maybe William Miller figured it out. Young Lisa Clark never did.

However, this early failure in my potentially prophetic career did not cause any sort of crisis of faith for me. I simply assumed it was a matter of time before the best Adventist theologians wrote some good books on the subject. For me, being an Adventist meant knowing the answers to everything. To put it bluntly, I was more interested in being right, in having the facts, in knowing something that other people didn't know, than in knowing Jesus and looking forward to spending time with Him. For me, learning to be a follower of Jesus and seeing His coming as the ultimate breaking through of the kingdom of God that He declared, came later. *After* learning the data, the rationale, the facts about the truths of the Bible and being able to explain them to other Christians. *After* learning that sometimes I've even been mistaken in my own ideas and theological explanations.

The journey to a trusting faith experience, a "second naivety"—a Jesus-loves-me-this-I-know, profound desire to partake of that love with others—was a gradual process. Education, life experience, deep relationships with others were all required to bring me to this point. And it takes even more love and patience to keep me here. We don't always have to choose between having Jesus and being right. But we should be sure which one is most important to us.

After disappointment

The aftermath of the Great Disappointment in 1844 was a crucible for many young Christians trying to sort out what really counted for them—what they had truly been staking their claim on. Contemporaries of William Miller noted that he had been hesitant to call his predictions "demonstrated facts"—that he always used words like "probably" when discussing what he considered to be the most reliable conclusions based on his careful study.[2] Most of all, he wanted to meet his Savior, and this was also the case with so many of his readers and listeners.

Jesus in Our History

One participant in the Advent movement recalled:

> Thousands of believers in Christ . . . manifest their entire confidence that their Savior was about to visit them in person and take them to his eternal abode. . . . [T]here was a nearness of approach to God and a sweetness of communion with Him, to which those who experienced it will ever recur with pleasure.[3]

For Miller, as for Joshua Himes, who was also one of the primary voices of the early Advent movement, Jesus came first. They really believed that good ideas mattered, but the desire to know and understand truth came out of the desire to know Jesus. And so Miller held the data, the rationale, the proof texts, lightly in his hands.

The language of the Bridegroom was crucial—they were waiting for Jesus to come, and when He didn't come at the exact predicted moment, they were *still* sure He would be coming personally—and soon—so they continued to wait for Him, "occupying."

Himes wrote after the Disappointment: "We have found the grace of God sufficient to sustain us. We have fled to His mercy and grace through Jesus Christ. Our hearts have been inspired with tender sympathy for each other." God's people, he asserted, should continue to wait for Him and be comforted by Him, through the love of Jesus.[4] James White remembered Miller as having rebuked people for squabbling over exactly where they went wrong with the prophecies, saying that it would be a shame for Jesus to come back—as He still doubtless would—and find them engaged in such petty arguing.[5]

> The language of the Bridegroom was crucial—they were waiting for Jesus to come.

Clearly, the early Adventists often attracted people who were very impressed with the correctness of the theology. They were Christians, but the new information presented by William Miller regarding the soon and personal coming of Jesus both added to and changed their faith. Depending on their temperaments and particulars of their life experiences, the details of the prophecies of Daniel and Revelation brought to their minds a sense of excitement about the world made new, a concern about judgment for sin, and a deep passion for getting ready to meet Jesus. Some were people we're happy to have in our heritage; some were frankly unbalanced and brought shame on their colleagues, both at the time and in historical memory.

The First True Thing

For many, like Miller and Himes, the news that Jesus would come soon *followed* a conversion experience and built on it. For others, such as the young Ellen Harmon, a conversion experience followed the desire to be right, precise, fact-based. Later, Ellen Harmon White would tell her story in a way that she hoped would influence the others who had experienced what she had or those who would come to join the fledgling movement that grew out of the Great Disappointment. As a young girl hearing the Milllerite message, the judgment that would occur at Jesus' return was the main thing that she thought about, until at one of the meetings, she was praying for relief from her sins. Later she wrote about that moment,

> It seemed that heaven opened and Jesus seemed very near to me; I felt able to come to Him with all my grief's misfortunes and trials, even as needy ones came to Him for relief when He was upon earth. There was a surety in my heart that He understood my peculiar trials and sympathized with me. . . . One of the mothers in Israel came to me and said, "Dear child, have you found Jesus?" I was about to answer "Yes" when she exclaimed, "Indeed you have; His peace is with you, I see it in your face!"[6]

From that point on, for White, the waiting was for Jesus, and the time was filled with affection for her fellow believers and a sense of closeness to their Creator God and Savior. She said she wished that the truth of Jesus' love had been shared with her as the primary thing to be sought after. For her and those who were blessed by her pastoral leadership, the Disappointment was made more endurable by her early vision of Jesus leading His people along the path to the New Jerusalem. She later wrote:

It was hard to take up the cares of life that we thought had been laid down forever. It was a bitter disappointment that fell upon the little flock whose faith had been so strong and whose hope had been so high. But we were surprised that we felt so free in the Lord and were so strongly sustained by His strength and grace.[7]

That vision of Jesus leading His people so tenderly became the symbol of their First True Thing, their highest priority.

Having the Truth

For White and her fellow Adventists, especially those who became the Seventh-day Adventists, being right and precise about prophecy, about the truth of Daniel and Revelation and the coming of Jesus, was important. But everyone knew how wrong they all had been. They lost a great deal of truth credibility. They were made fun of and literally persecuted in their communities. It was humbling and upsetting to be so very mistaken. And when they found that out, what saved them, what helped them through, what was always at the heart of it, was that Jesus was with them. Being wrong gave them a chance to emphasize how important the presence and love of Jesus in the Body of Christ, through the power of the Holy Spirit, was to them.

> What helped them through, what was always at the heart of it, was that Jesus was with them.

Because the truth isn't a "what." It's a Who. For those who made it through this disappointment, it was the Jesus they knew, the Jesus who was close to them and comforted them, the Jesus who was the center of their world, who made sense of it all for them. Now, this is really *really* hard for someone like me. I get paid to contribute to correct understanding. Concern for right thinking and correct information is at the core of my temperament and my profession. I evaluate people on whether they are right—and I'm *supposed* to be right about facts, about data.

To say that Jesus is all I need is very scary for me. I'm worried about what someone is going to go do with that. I'm worried about incorrect ideas of who God is and what He wants for us prejudicing people against Him or leading people down the wrong path. Someone says "Just focus on Jesus—He's all that matters" and I want to say, "Yes, but can we have a conversation about what your theological understanding of the Incarnation is? You do understand what we ultimately mean when we talk about Jesus, right?" I want to add to it. It is scary for me to rely on just Jesus, and to trust others to rely on Him, too.

And yet this is my heritage. This is where we started. This is what the church has been doing since His crucifixion. This is where my own stream of Christianity started—waiting with bated breath for their Jesus to break through personally. They wanted to touch Him, to drink the new wine with Him as He had promised, to say goodbye to sin and death and all that He had conquered by His life and resurrection.

If William Miller is a great example of someone who started out with a deep conversion, then sought to be theologically correct out of that experience, Ellen White represents those who started out wanting to be right, then learned to love Jesus. Her ideas of what truth was gradually grew into ever more Christ-shaped images because of this—and because, for her, Jesus was always at the center. And the Disappointment only brought this home more clearly for her and for her loved ones.

Being wrong together

This Disappointment, this being wrong about something, wasn't the end of the story for this community of believers. What comforted them, helped them heal, helped them move forward, was coming together in the Body of Christ. Confessing their grief, their anxiety, their mistakes together, in the Presence of Jesus made real in the Spirit in the gathering of the saints—this was the starting place.

It wasn't the last time they would have to say they had made an error. Sadly, even this very gathering and comforting of each other and loving Jesus as the Bridegroom and promising to continue to wait for Him, prompted some to say that it was too late for anyone else to claim

Jesus in Our History

Jesus as their Bridegroom. The parable was so real for them and they identified so much with the five virgins waiting behind that closed door for the wedding party (see Matthew 25:1–13) that they started to see everyone who was not gathered with them as outcast. This became known as the "Shut Door" theology. Out of their pain and group unity and passion for Jesus came a sense of exclusivity. While this false idea was not held by all the young Adventists, it still had to be confessed and repented of.

Even in all this, Jesus remained present with them, drawing them to Himself, teaching them how to love better. And it is quite a heritage to stand on—to be part of a church whose beginnings are rooted not in a raw doctrinal certainty, but in a powerful knowledge that they were loved by Jesus and that He was both with them and coming again.

So we gather together and remember those whose first reaction, both to the anticipation of His coming and to the disappointment at its delay, was to come together with others who loved Jesus and to tell their stories. We stand in a tradition whose founding moment was a confession that Jesus was true and faithful, even though they were broken and confused. They gathered in their brokenness and loved each other, prayed for each other and worshiped Jesus, and as they worshipped Him and loved each other—He was there.

> Out of their pain and group unity and passion for Jesus came a sense of exclusivity.

He is with us

I need this gathering. I need this broken Body of Christ. I need your love for me and I need to practice loving you, because alone I too often become more and more sure of myself. Pride in being right is one of my particular sins. I need to confess my sins and be forgiven, and to practice forgiveness of you and your weaknesses in my turn. The heritage of the Adventist community is a long one for learning to forgive and to practice loving broken people, of confessing our mistakes and the fact that our mistakes all too often cause us to put up barriers to loving others.

For the One

And we keep waiting for His kingdom to fully break through. Because we love Him and keep making Him our center, we keep gathering to tell our stories of what He has done for us. We do this, building on a heritage of those who had a profound experience of Jesus, sought understanding of Him in the Scriptures, and attempted to articulate it, announce it, and even found comfort when they were wrong. They were able to continue reformulating their understanding because of His amazing love, the strong sense of His forgiveness, and the joy and strength they received from others who loved Him.

When we are wrong, Jesus is still with us.

When we thought we knew what it meant to follow Him and it all blows up in our face, He is beside us.

When we've staked our claim on something, then fall on our face in front of everyone, Jesus is still there.

And when we gather with our fellow believers, confessing our sins, hearing each other's stories, sharing each other's heartbreaks—then, most of all, Jesus is here.

---

1. Sylvester Bliss, *Memoirs of William Miller,* Joshua Himes, Boston, 1853, pages 66, 67.

2. Isaac Wellcome, *History of the Second Advent Message and People,* Advent Christian Publishing Society, Boston, 1874, page 336.

3. ibid, page 365.

4. David Arthur, "Joshua V Himes and the Cause of Adventism" in Numbers and Butler, *The Disappointed*, University of Tennessee Press, Knoxville, TN, 1993, pages 52, 53.

5. James White, *Sketches of The Christian Life and Public Labors of William Miller*, Steam Press, Battle Creek, MI, 1875, page 332.

6. Ellen White, *Life Sketches of Ellen G White*, page 23.

7. Ellen White, *Testimonies for the Church, Volume 1*, page 56.

"An unutterable yearning"
Why 1888 matters to Adventists today

Sam Leonor

I imagine it as a beautiful Michigan fall morning. James White leaned back in his chair and made a decision. It wasn't a decision made by a committee, task force, board, council, commission, group or team. He just made a decision.

In 1880, James White wrote this simple but profound statement: "I have an unutterable yearning of the soul for Christ."

Only a year before his death at the age of 60, he was in his last year as president of the General Conference of Seventh-day Adventists, a denomination that had officially existed for a mere 17 years. He was one of our founders, serving as president while under the debilitating effects of a stroke he had suffered 15 years earlier at the age of only 44, likely from overworking himself and neglecting his health.

I think that in his study that morning he had such a desire for Jesus: "I have an unutterable yearning of the soul for Christ."

And I'm sure he began to ask questions:

How did we go from being a people with one overwhelming, all-consuming, irrepressible, irresistible, overpowering, and radical desire to be with Jesus—finding Jesus in every page of scripture—to the kind of people who spent more time and energy arguing with each other over

For the One

whether the 10th horn of Daniel 7:24 represents the Huns or Alemani tribes? Or more time, resources and energy—brutalizing each other—over whether the "law" in Galatians was ceremonial or moral?

How did we go from being a people who proclaimed the good news that the Bridegroom is coming—with hearts full of joy!—to doing evangelism this way:

- An Adventist evangelist would move into a town, identify the most prominent clergy and challenge him to a public debate.

THE WAY OF LIFE
FROM PARADISE LOST TO PARADISE RESTORED.

Often using this beautiful drawing—that James White had commissioned—the evangelist would "prove" the Sabbath, the state of the dead, Bible prophecy and the importance of the law. According to history I've read, we were unbeatable. We would assault people with the truth. A reporter for a secular newspaper wrote, "The Adventists argue theology with about the same industry that an earnest man with a hatchet would assail a cord of wood."

But, in this picture, where was the cross of Jesus? It's like playing an Adventist version of "Where's Waldo?" James realized we were creating a church full of people who were right, but not necessarily Christian. When you fill a church with people who were won over with a better argument, don't be surprised if what they most love to do is argue.

All of this left James—and others—with "an unutterable yearning of the soul for Christ."

Something happened to James. He knew this church didn't belong to him, it belongs to Jesus. James also knew his life was soon coming to an end, and he looked at his little flock and realized they had to be led to Jesus.

A friend wrote this about his preaching in the last year of his life: "Wherever he preached the past few months, he dwelt almost solely upon faith in Christ and His boundless love for us."

So the decision he made that morning in Michigan, a year before his death? He commissioned a new drawing with the cross of Jesus now dominating the center. He wrote this appeal to the church: "Christ should be lifted up in all His exceeding loveliness and power as 'God with us' that His attractiveness may thus draw all unto Him."

CHRIST, THE WAY OF LIFE

This movement he and others were setting in motion in the young Adventist denomination would be faced with many questions, accusations and assumptions. But can you hear—and see—this yearning of the soul?

Enter the Californians

In 1882, a medical doctor by the name of E J Waggoner, who had left his medical practice to pursue ministry, was at a camp meeting in Healdsburg, California, when he had an experience he described this way:

A light shone around me, and the tent was, for me, far

more brilliantly lighted than if the noonday sun had been shinning, and I saw Christ hanging on the cross, crucified for me. In that moment I had my first positive knowledge, which came like an overwhelming flood, that God loved me, and that Christ died for me. . . . Since then wherever I have turned in the Bible, I have found Christ set forth as the power of God . . . and I have never found anything else.

What was happening with Waggoner? Were these people crazy? Did they really have weird mystical experiences, rendering their testimony suspect? Was it from eating big meals before they went to sleep? "The tent was shinning like . . ."

Yes, crazy—but maybe only as crazy as this Jewish writer: "We have seen his glory, glory as of the only Son from the Father, full of grace and truth" (John 1:14).

Or crazy like this story in Acts 9: "Suddenly a light from heaven shone around him. And falling to the ground he heard a voice saying to him, 'Saul, Saul, why are you persecuting me?'" (Acts 9:3, 4).

Another of those "crazy" Californians was A T Jones, a former military sergeant who had spent his years in the army reading history and theology that had led him to a profound love for Jesus. Discharged from the army in 1873, he found these peculiar people—the Adventist church—who understood prophecy and history the way he had come to understand it, And they were expecting the soon-coming of Jesus. It seemed perfect!

But soon he realized that many Adventists suffered from a condition we only recently have a name for: Jesus-Deficit Disorder. This law-oriented Adventism left Jones cold. He couldn't reconcile this with the Jesus he had met in scripture and in his personal study.

James and Ellen White, Jones, Waggoner and others: they weren't crazy. They had seen the glory of the One. They had come alive.

The majority

But they would need to be ready to swim against the current. The majority of the church was led by George Butler and Uriah Smith and let's just say they weren't having it:

George Butler was president of the General Conference in the lead up to 1888. He opposed this "Jesus before all things" message. He asserted that being president of the church gave him "clearer views than others on doctrinal issues."

Uriah Smith had been editor of the *Advent Review and Sabbath Herald* almost continuously since 1855. For some time, he had also served as secretary of the church. He was an authority on Bible prophecy and strongly opposed what he called the "Western Conspiracy." Earlier in 1888, Smith published this statement in reaction to Jones and Waggoner: "Adventists have never taken a stand upon Bible exegesis which they have been compelled to surrender." Perhaps it was convenient for him to ignore the disappointment of 1844, the early Adventists' "Shut Door" theology and Arianism heresy.

Waggoner's response was profound. "A change in our position would simply say that Adventists are better informed today than they were yesterday," he wrote.

But these leaders and the majority they represented weren't ignorant or evil. Instead, I think they were distracted by a few things:

- In 1888, the end of days was here. Adventists were serving time in chain gangs for breaking Sunday laws. Even Ellen White's son, Willie, had been arrested in California for operating the Pacific Press on Sunday. And then the big one: on May 21, 1888, New Hampshire senator H W Blair introduced a national "Sunday law" bill—the first since the inception of the Adventist movement. It was an emotional time. They believed they were living at the very end of time! All that they had been teaching for 40 years was about to come to pass. And it is difficult to convince people who are serving time on chain gangs for keeping the Sabbath that the law is less important than Jesus.

- They were also distracted by the desire to keep power and there were some strong personalities on both sides of this divide, which did not help resolve the situation. These new guys were making it sound like they didn't love Jesus. But because the established leaders

> "A change in our position would simply say that Adventists are better informed today than they were yesterday."

For the One

had been around for 40 years by this time, their faith had matured and they had found other things to occupy themselves with while they waited for the Second Coming, such as learning how to live right. To them, it wasn't legalism. But the new generation sure experienced it that way.

The 1888 conference

In the lead-up to the 1888 conference, Ellen White wrote, "The world should no longer say that Adventists talk the law, the law, but do not teach or believe Christ." She urged church leaders and conference participants to listen to Jones and Waggoner.

From 1884 to 1887, Ellen White had been a neutral mediator but she shifted her position to open advocacy for the message Jones and Waggoner brought. She made room for them and protected them in the face of attack.

In October, 1888, they gathered in Minneapolis. Butler stayed away, becoming physically ill after receiving such a severe rebuke from Ellen White. But Uriah Smith and their supporters came ready for battle.

Here are some short descriptions of the meeting from people who were "tweeting" reports from the conference:
- "The discourses are Christ-less."
- "There was much disrespect of brother towards brother."
- "Hurtful speeches were made against Elder Jones and Waggoner."
- "The spirit of Minneapolis is synonymous with the spirit of disharmony."

Ellen White wrote that "Jesus was grieved and bruised by His saints." This is something we are still doing in our church arguments today. Although with the internet, now we can do it on a larger scale and often with the cloak of invisibility. Even when our disagreements seem fundamental to us . . . Jesus is bruised and grieved.

But something happened in Minneapolis toward the end of the meeting. Jesus appeared. His glory was seen.

Waggoner concluded his last sermon by saying this: "The everlasting gospel is the message of the three angels, Jesus, crucified, living, and coming again. We have nothing else in this world to proclaim."

There—yearning in his soul for Christ.

After 1888

After the meetings, Ellen White became the most vocal supporter of the Jesus message championed by Jones and Waggoner. She called their message "a most precious message," a message that "was to bring more prominently before the world the uplifted Savior, the sacrifice for the sins of the whole world. It presented justification through faith in the Surety; it invited the people to receive the righteousness of Christ."

Her open support and advocacy for their message earned her a trip to Australia. She was 65—and she didn't want to go. But she was sent away by the church leaders who were smarting from their "defeat" at the Minneapolis conference and were looking to re-assert their authority.

Yet, in Australia, Ellen White wrote only about Jesus. From 1888 until her death, she tried to lead the church to Jesus, producing many of her best-loved books: *Steps to Christ* (1892), *Thoughts from the Mount of Blessing* (1896), *The Desire of Ages* (1898), *Christ's Object Lessons* (1900) and *The Ministry of Healing* (1905).

As Adventists, we are Christians largely because of that 1888 conference.

And more than 120 years later, like James White, we have felt the same unutterable yearning of the soul for Christ. We want to know Jesus in all of His glory and be captivated by His beauty and love. So that like our pioneers we may also say with confidence that the most important message we have to proclaim is Jesus—crucified, living and coming again.

> As Adventists, we are Christians largely because of that 1888 conference.

Deep Water

Being amazed by Jesus

Emily Whitney

A friend recently shared with me a little book of poetry. Author Ann Weems writes about her faith experience in church and her journey with God. As I read this book, there was a passage that I found myself reading again and again:

> Here's the Church, and here's the steeple.
> Open the door. Where are the people? . . .
>
> He is risen! He who was dead is alive, but
> we who say we believe continue our quarreling,
> Flipping through Bibles to find passages
> To support our private theologies.
> No wonder the children have left!
> We forgot to teach them the story.
> We taught moralisms instead of the Word of God.
> We've put Jesus back in the tomb, rolled the stone back in
>   place, and
> Continued to behave as though he is dead.
> Have we not heard? Have we not known?
> Yes, we have heard; yes, we have known,
> But our hearts are hardened.
> We hoard our stars and store up treasures here on earth . . .
>
> Anxious and stressed, vying for positions and power,
> We spend our energies creating more rules,
> For fear of losing control,
> The rules have become more important
> Than the freeing word of God.

Jesus in Our History

> We have processed the gospel into neat
> little packages and stacks of paper.
> We've gathered the saints into committees
> and asked them to serve without starlight.
> We've drained the poetry from the gospel.
> We've taken the amazing out of grace
> And the glory out of God.[1]

Ann Weems is talking about her experience in the Presbyterian faith, but could her words ring true for Adventism as well? Sadly, I think they do. I know as I read these words they lay heavy on my heart. I wondered if, as Seventh-day Adventists, we have "taken the amazing out of grace and the glory out of God." Have we lost our sense of amazement, our wonder at the mystery of Jesus? And, if so, how do we recapture this sense of amazement and wonder?

There is no better place to turn in scripture in a quest for amazement than the gospel of Luke, described by one commentator as "the gospel of amazement." While other gospel writers might use one Greek form of this word, Luke uses all five possible Greek words.[2] You will see this word translated in several different ways as people encounter Jesus. They are in awe, they are astounded, they are awestruck, and they are amazed.

A story of amazement

The story told in Luke 5:1–11 is a story of amazement. Jesus was walking by the lake when He met Simon and some of the others. They were washing their nets after an unsuccessful night's fishing and Jesus borrowed their boat as a platform to address the crowd, before suggesting the fishermen try one more time. Reluctantly, Simon agreed to Jesus' request:

> When they had done this, they enclosed a large number of fish, and their nets were breaking. They signaled to their partners in the other boat to come and help them. And they came and filled both the boats, so that they began to sink. But when Simon Peter saw it, he fell down at Jesus' knees, saying, "Depart from me, for I am a sinful man, O Lord."

For the One

> For he and all who were with him were astonished at the catch of fish that they had taken, and so also were James and John, sons of Zebedee, who were partners with Simon. And Jesus said to Simon, "Do not be afraid; from now on you will be catching men." And when they had brought their boats to land, they left everything and followed him (Luke 5:6–11).

This was not the first time Simon had encountered Jesus. Their first meeting is recorded in John 1. Simon's brother Andrew encountered Jesus and told Simon he had met the Messiah. Andrew brought Simon to meet Jesus, and Jesus and Simon talked face to face. Jesus even told Simon that his name would change to Simon Peter.

Despite this first meeting, we come to Luke 5 and Simon was still about his own business. He was not yet a disciple. He had not yet left everything to follow Jesus. Simon might have been able to tell us a lot about Jesus. He might have confessed that Jesus was the Messiah. In Luke 5, Simon even addressed Jesus as "Rabbi"—as one with authority. But Simon was not yet a disciple. Maybe this was because Simon was not yet amazed by Jesus.

These two meetings between Simon and Jesus send a warning to my heart and mind because it tells me that we can know a lot about Jesus. We can meet Jesus. We can encounter Jesus. We may even say He is the One. However, it doesn't mean we have set out to follow Him, left everything to follow Him. It doesn't mean we are disciples. It doesn't mean we have ever truly been amazed by Jesus. So I ask myself and I ask you: Are you more like Simon before his encounter with Jesus in Luke 5 or after? Are we—as a church—more like Simon before or after he was amazed?

A progressive calling

One thing I love about this story is how Jesus progressively calls Simon. When we meet Jesus in Luke 5, He was preaching to a crowd of people. Jesus then preached from Simon's boat. Jesus intentionally addressed Simon, asking him to push off a little from the shoreline. I imagine that, to do so, Simon might have gotten into the boat. Jesus had now moved Simon from the safety of the shore to the shallow waters.

Jesus in Our History

As Jesus finished preaching, He again turned to Simon and now called him to "put out into the deep." Jesus loves to call His people deeper. No longer could Simon stay on the shore, and no longer could he rest in the security of the shallows. Jesus had something more, something deeper for Simon—something amazing.

Jesus told Simon to put out into the deep and lower his nets for a catch. But nothing about this request made any sense to Simon the fisherman. Jesus, the carpenter, was telling this fisherman how to fish. And Simon did what is so humanly natural, he began to tell Jesus all that he knew: "Jesus, this just isn't going to work. We have fished all night and caught nothing." Simon was telling Jesus that what He asked simply wasn't going to work.

To Simon's credit, he obeyed the call of Jesus, despite his objections. However, in my imagining of the story, Simon responded with a bit of haughty confidence, "because you say so" (Luke 5:5). I don't hear this as a faith statement but with more of an air of "You'll see, Jesus. I'll show you that you are wrong."

Yet Simon pushed out into the deep, let down the nets for a catch and, to his amazement, boatloads of fish filled the nets. Beyond Simon's imagining, beyond his understanding, Jesus did something amazing.

> Beyond Simon's imagining, beyond his understanding, Jesus did something amazing.

At this moment of amazement, we see a transition. Simon was transformed. His response to Jesus was no longer of haughty confidence but a humble confession. And Jesus called him deeper still, not to the deep waters of a lake but to the deep waters of the world. Jesus always calls His disciples deeper.

Pushing out into the deep shows us more of Jesus. It is in the deep waters of the uncomfortable and unknown where we are amazed by the wonder and mystery that is Jesus. And in knowing Him more fully, we are transformed. It is in the deep water where Jesus continually calls us deeper still.

In our history

As a people of faith, we are here today because our forefathers and

For the One

mothers of the faith were people who launched out into the deep waters of scripture, who decided their knowledge and understanding of Jesus was not enough. They wanted more of Jesus. Because men and women risked such depths, we have the truths we follow today. Because they ventured into the deep of scripture, we have this great belief called "present truth," meaning we have the expectation that there is always more of Jesus to be revealed and to experience. Like Simon's encounter with Jesus, as we progressively go deeper with Jesus, He opens greater, deeper realities and revelations of Himself.

A wonderful example of this, one of my favorites in our church history, is what happened in 1888. It's fascinating to me that we actually argued over righteousness by faith. But sadly we did. A T Jones and E J Waggoner ventured into the deep as they studied righteousness by faith and as they presented it in 1888. As a church, we entered into the deep waters of the uncomfortable and the unknown. However, what was revealed was wonderfully more of Jesus and deeper understanding.

I love what George Knight writes about this experience in his book called *Anticipating the Advent*. He writes, "Up until this time we had two parts of a three-part message in Revelation 14:12," referring to "the patience of the saints," awaiting the second coming of Jesus, and our striving to be those who "keep the commandments of God," particularly in the truth of the Sabbath. But it was not until 1888 that we got the "faith of Jesus Christ." Knight goes on to say, "The significance of the 1888 meetings is that Adventists were baptized anew into Christianity."[3]

Because of 1888, we are Christians:

> The distinct pillar doctrines were infused with the Holy Spirit. Adventists, at least some of them, finally understood the entire Third Angel's Message. From that point on we could preach a full message that taught the distinct Adventist doctrines within the larger context of the saving work of Christ. Because of this, with this full message and this new understanding of faith in Jesus, we then became, in the next decade, a worldwide denomination.[4]

As a church we went into deep water of the unknown and found more of Jesus and the truth of righteousness by faith. We went into deep water and we received, to our amazement, more of Jesus. And in receiving more of Jesus, our commission and our realities as a church broadened to the entire world.

More of Jesus

I love my church. I am a born-and-raised Seventh-day Adventist, a product of Adventist education, and I am privileged and honored to serve in the church that I love. But I'm disappointed sometimes—heartbroken, even—when we speak as if there is nothing else to learn, when we speak, like Peter, with haughty confidence.

This disturbs me so deeply because, if we think we know all there is to know, then we might miss the "more of Jesus" He wants to reveal. I love my church and I believe we still serve the same Jesus who called Simon deeper, who called our mothers and fathers of faith deeper still.

Deep water can be scary because it is uncertain and unknown. Knowing this, Jesus often prefaced His callings with the words "Do not fear; do not be afraid." God always repeats this when He calls His people to big, grand, amazing things: "Do not be afraid."

> God always repeats this when He calls His people to big, grand, amazing things: "Do not be afraid."

However, I think there is a healthy fear we should have. I wonder what would have been different in Simon's life if he hadn't gone deeper. What would have happened if after being amazed by Jesus, Simon had said, "That is enough of Jesus"? What if as a church we didn't have mothers and fathers of the faith who dug deeper into the Word of God? What if we never wrestled with righteousness by faith? What deeper revelations of Jesus might we miss if—in fear—we do not venture into the deep water where He is calling us?

I know Jesus—I have encountered Him—but I want more and more of Him. I am not ready to say, "I have enough Jesus." I want more of Jesus. And I want more of Him for my church. I want more of Him for you and for me. I want more of Jesus. If discovering more of Jesus

For the One

means plunging into uncomfortable and unknown deep waters, then let's be uncomfortable, let's risk it, because it is there in the deep waters where amazement is found. There in the deep waters we discover more of Jesus.

The present question remains: What is the deep water to which Jesus is calling us, as individuals and as a church?

As we venture into the deep waters with Jesus, the longing of my heart is found in the words of the hymn "More about Jesus I would know." May it be the heartbeat of our church—and the song of our hearts:

> More about Jesus let me learn,
> More of His holy will discern;
> Spirit of God, my teacher be,
> Showing the things of Christ to me.
>
> More, more about Jesus,
> More, more about Jesus;
> More of His saving fullness see,
> More of His love who died for me.[5]

---

1. Ann Weems, *Putting the Amazing Back in Grace*, Westminster John Knox Press, 1999, pages 20–22.

2. Michael Card, *Luke: The Gospel of Amazement*, IVP Press, 2011.

3. George Knight, *A Brief History of Seventh-day Adventists*, Review and Herald, 2000, page 93.

4. George Knight, *Anticipating the Advent: A Brief History of Seventh-Day Adventists*, Pacific Press, 1993, page 73.

5. Eliza Hewitt (1887), "More About Jesus," *Seventh-day Adventist Hymnal*, #245.

Jesus in Our Theology

Jesus. Doctrine.

Jesus and our beliefs

Mark Witas

"Doctrine" is such a cold-sounding word.

To some, it sounds like a swear word: "Oh yeah! Well, you're full of *Doctrine!*"

Doctrine: it might sound like a place where good ideas go to die.

I can't tell you how many times I've had church members ask me, "Why do we have 28 fundamental beliefs? Are there exactly 28 things we are supposed to believe in? What if I'm only invested in 25 of them; do I still belong?" 25 out of 28 is 89 per cent. That's a strong B+! Can I be a good Adventist with a B+? Does 89 per cent of Adventist doctrine get you into heaven?

Such comments reflect my experience that many in the Seventh-day Adventist Church view our doctrine as a collection of beliefs that define us and separate us from "Babylon." But this is a gross misunderstanding of what doctrine is for.

Rather than our doctrine being used to define us as a church, our doctrine ought to be a biblical expression of the God we believe in. I think this particular view is more relevant than ever to the Seventh-day Adventist Church and its members today. Let me explain by retelling a story you are familiar with. It's called "The Great Controversy."

Revisiting the story

A long, long time ago, far, far away, the Bible says there was a war in heaven. But this was not a physically violent war. This war was a political war—a war of ideas and philosophy. The Bible says the Dragon that initiated this war was dragging God's name through the mud, trying to elevate himself above the God who created him. This war earned

For the One

Satan and his angels a ticket out of heaven.

Then, one day as Eve was walking through the garden, the snake in the tree said, "Did God really tell you not to eat from this tree?" In other words, *Who is God to tell you what to do? Who made Him the boss of you?* Eve began to question God's authority.

The snake-dragon continued his onslaught, "God said you would die if you eat the fruit? You will not surely die." The idea was put in Eve's head: *Maybe God isn't trustworthy. Maybe He's a liar.*

And then the final blow, "If you eat the fruit you will be just like God, knowing good from evil." Eve's mind was reeling now: *Is God holding out on me? Is God not giving me what I should rightfully have?*

Eve used to think that the tree was bad and that God was good. Now she saw the tree as good, and God as bad. In deceiving Adam and Eve, the dragon warped the human idea about God.

As Revelation 12:9 explains it, "And the great dragon was thrown down, that ancient serpent, who is called the devil and Satan, the deceiver of the whole world—he was thrown down to the earth, and his angels were thrown down with him." Scripture tells us that the dragon intends to deceive the whole world about who God is. His plan was successful in the garden.

But God had a plan. God raised up a people to represent Him on earth. He chose a people, the seed of Abraham to learn of Him, know Him and shine as a light to the whole world—to show and tell the world the truth about a loving God. Israel was to reveal the Father to the world. In Hosea 11:1, Israel is referred to as the "son" of God.

But, as Israel developed their cult of worship and their doctrine, they fell into the horrible trap of having their doctrine define and separate them as a people instead of letting their doctrine point to and speak of a God of grace who wants to bless, redeem and save. Anytime a group of people use doctrine to define themselves rather than establishing doctrine to explain and clarify God, they will yield to the real temptation of considering themselves separate from and better than the rest of the world. And this will ultimately do damage to God's character, no matter what truth they may possess.

Thus, Israel did damage to God's character. But God had a plan. God wanted to be reconciled to His people. He wanted people to know who

He truly is. So the mystery of God was revealed when God put on flesh and became a man.

Jesus the doctrine

Jesus was given the same task as Israel, to clarify the Father. And He was also called God's son. John 1:18 says, "No-one has seen God at any time; the only begotten God who is in the bosom of the Father, He has explained *Him*."

Even with all of the books of the Old Testament, God's people had a very warped idea of who He was. So Jesus came to explain the Father.

Jesus said, "Whoever has seen me has seen the Father" (John 14:9). More than anything or anyone else in the history of the world, Jesus is the revelation of the true character of God. Jesus became the doctrine of God in the flesh.

And notice the differences between Jesus' representations of the Father and how the doctrine of the "church" in Jesus' day defined Him.

- Jesus took the nature of a servant. God's church lorded over their people and looked down on the world.
- Jesus mixed with sinners. God's people shunned them.
- Jesus included and redeemed. The church separated itself and condemned—in the name of God.

Instead of showing the world the love of the Father, the doctrine of Israel ended up alienating and separating. Jesus had to come to become doctrine in flesh.

So when Jesus went back to heaven to sit at the right-hand side of the Father, He handed the responsibility of revealing the Father to us, His church. He left us—the sons and daughters of God—in charge of revealing the Father to a dying world.

Church and doctrine

For the One

But history tells us that it wasn't long before the church started going down the same road as the nation of Israel had done before them. It wasn't long before the church warped and perverted God's character.

The church became rich and self-absorbed. It began to use force instead of love. It started to teach things about God that created a gulf between the Father and His people.

Instead of focusing on the life, death and resurrection of Jesus, the church began to create doctrine to define and separate itself again. The church began to use doctrine to impose its will and to try to spiritually control people. It used fear as a tactic to manipulate and control.

- It began to teach things like, "God loves you. But if you don't love Him back, He'll get angry and throw you into an ever-burning inferno, torturing you for all eternity."
- It began to teach that God is unapproachable, that instead of going to God with your burdens, you had to go to a priest, or to Mary, or to a dead saint.
- They started to teach that babies were born lost and that if you didn't baptize them shortly after birth, they'd suffer an eternity in hell if they died.
- They started offering forgiveness for money, and the ability to sin and not be held accountable—for a price.
- They elevated human teachings and traditions above the will of God as written in the Holy Scriptures.
- And if you didn't agree with the church's doctrine? Economic sanctions, imprisonment or death by fire while tied to a stake.

Jesus saw what His church would one day become. In John 16:2, Jesus says, "They will put you out of the synagogues. Indeed, the hour is coming when whoever kills you will think he is offering service to God."

Is it possible to be so blinded by your own doctrine that you would actually take human life in God's name and think you are doing Him a service?

Particularly during the Middle Ages—but also at many other times throughout Christian history—God's church has failed miserably at letting Jesus' life, death and resurrection define its doctrine. Instead, it used doctrine as a way to coerce people and manipulate them to act like they wanted them to act.

The great danger of doctrine is that it can be used to manipulate people to join a church, to stay in a church, to contribute to a church, or to define a church. To borrow from the description in Revelation, doctrine can cause a church to look like the lamb, but speak and act like the dragon.

Another church?

I believe strongly that this is where the prophetic calling of the Seventh-day Adventist Church comes into play. The primary purpose of this movement is to tell the world the truth about God—to dispel the false picture of God that the church has saturated the world with for centuries. The books of Daniel and Revelation prophesy about the rise of a people who would be given the task of cleaning up the lies about God that the church has littered the world with.

Our church had an awkward beginning. We grew out of a movement that was dead wrong about the dates and times of Jesus' return. But out of that great disappointment and gross error grew a people devoted to voraciously studying the Bible and banking on being with Jesus as soon as He would allow.

> It turned out that God wasn't the aloof tyrant the church had painted Him to be . . . God was a lot more like Jesus.

As they developed into an actual movement—into a church—they discovered things in the Bible that nobody else was teaching about God. It turned out that God wasn't the aloof tyrant the church had painted Him to be, running hot and cold in His feelings toward us. In fact, God was a lot more like Jesus.

So, through much study, our evolving church began to establish doctrine. Through the years, this has been a good thing—and this has been a bad thing. It was a good thing in that our doctrine painted a beautiful picture of God who, as it turns out, is just like Jesus. But, in our history, we have not always used or taught doctrine well.

A doctrine of family

For the One

My mom is an atheist. She doesn't believe in God.

My mom grew up in the Seventh-day Adventist Church at a time when I believe people used doctrine to define and separate the church, instead of using doctrine to reveal the grace of God through Jesus Christ.

As she grew up, my mother had the sanctuary doctrine explained like this: starting in 1844, God opened up some books. In one of those books is your name. When He gets to your name, He is going to look at your life to see if you still struggle with sin. If at that time you are still sinning, then "He who is filthy, let him be filthy still." If God doesn't see that you love Him enough to have stopped sinning, your name will be blotted out of the Book of Life and you won't be included in heaven. For you, probation will be closed.

By the time my mom was 14 years old, she'd made up her mind. She couldn't possibly reach that level of perfection. She didn't think it possible. There couldn't possibly be a God who would make getting to heaven so hard. So there must not be a God.

Five years later, when my mom was in college, she was driving home on a Sabbath afternoon to surprise her family. Her car broke down about 45 minutes from home, so she used a pay phone and called her father.

The response of her father, the faithful church member and beloved professor from La Sierra University? "You know how I feel about you travelling on Sabbath. I'll come get you after sundown."

She waited in her car in 90-degree weather for six hours until her father got there—after the family had sundown worship without her.

Is this what doctrine is supposed to be?

Jesus. Doctrine.

The challenge for the Seventh-day Adventist Church in the 21st century is to avoid using doctrine to define and separate ourselves. Instead, we need to make it clear that our doctrine describes Jesus as the revealer of God's character. If our doctrine doesn't clarify a loving God as displayed by Jesus while He was on earth, we need to re-look at our doctrine.

Do we celebrate the Sabbath as a gift from God that find's its fulfillment in Jesus? Or do we use it to separate ourselves from all those deceived people who have no idea they live in Babylon? Has the Sabbath become our Messiah or have we allowed the Messiah to become our Sabbath?

What would the Sabbath be without Jesus? Keeping the Sabbath and not believing in Jesus is tantamount to believing in the "state of the dead" without believing that Jesus will come and call us out of our graves.

Our calling as a church is not to create a set of doctrines that will separate us from a dying world. Our doctrine should send us into a dying world that is starving for the truth about God as seen in Jesus!

I believe that each doctrine this church holds dear is a wonderful revelation of God's character. I also believe that our church has sometimes yielded to the temptation to make our doctrines more about us than about our God. And I think that's one reason why there are more ex-Seventh-day Adventists than Seventh-day Adventists in the United States today.

We need to have strong biblical doctrine that reveals God as Jesus demonstrated Him in His life, death and resurrection. And if we use our doctrine or teach our doctrine in any other way, for any other purpose, we need to re-examine who we are as a church.

I love being a Seventh-day Adventist. I chose it . . . on purpose.

And I love what my church teaches about God.

But I fear that if we aren't careful, we can end up looking like a lamb and sounding like a dragon.

The statement of The One Project is "Jesus. All." But I would like to make another suggestion. How about "Jesus. Doctrine."?

> Our doctrine should send us into a dying world that is starving for the truth about God as seen in Jesus!

What is One?
Jesus' prayer for unity

Brandy Kirstein

When I was in seventh grade, my best friend and I would get up early to walk to school because we hated riding the bus. But, one morning, we were running late, so we had to take the bus. Our stop was one of the last, so all the seats were taken except for one. We wanted to sit together, so decided to sit there.

All at once, everyone started telling us we better move before the next stop because that was "Devin's seat."

"No," I said, "No-one gets their own seat. We all have to ride this bus and it's first come, first served."

They responded by warning me that Devin would beat me up.

Devin was an eighth grader who stood about a foot taller than most of the eighth-grade boys. She was a bully and always got her way.

But my stubbornness and pride kicked in and I replied, "Whatever. I'm from Vegas—OK, Bakersfield. I can handle this."

Next stop, Devin boarded the bus. She was a little bigger than I remembered, definitely could take an eighth-grade boy and definitely could take all scrawny, five-foot me.

She walked over and said, "Get out of my seat."

My friend started nudging me to get out of the seat. "No," I said.

"GET OUT OF MY SEAT," she said much more firmly.

"No," I replied, only slightly firm.

The bus driver then intervened and told Devin to sit down so we could get going. So she sat behind me and pulled my hair and swatted me most the way, while I stubbornly ignored her.

The next day, we rode the bus again. This time, my friend would not sit with me in "Devin's seat."

Devin boarded the bus and this time threatened me, "Move—or I'm going to beat you up at school."

"Devin," I told her, "Nobody has any more right to this seat than anyone else, including you, so you can do what you want, but as long as I get on this bus first, if this seat is available, then this is where I will sit. You can sit with me if you'd like."

Fire burned in her eyes, but again the bus driver intervened and made Devin sit down, so we could get going. She sat behind me and messed with me most of the way, while I proudly ignored her.

On the third day, history repeated itself. Everyone told me how stupid I was. The bus driver gave a sigh. My friend was not even sitting near me this time. And Devin said, "That's it. I've had enough of you. Today, I'm going to get you unless you GET OUT OF MY SEAT!"

The entire bus swarmed around us. I was completely terrified but would not move. I just looked straight ahead and ignored her as the bus driver came to the back and told her to sit in the front, and that we would talk about this when we arrived at school.

When we reached the school, the bus driver explained that if he heard of Devin touching me, he would make sure she was suspended or expelled from school. She had gotten in trouble a lot at school already and her "grace" was running out.

She would still pull my hair or push me down for a few weeks after when she saw me at school. But, by the end of the year, Devin told me that she respected me and we became a strange kind of friends.

Keeping the "peace"?

It is interesting that, even though everyone on the bus knew what Devin was doing was wrong and no-one liked it, they had agreed to allow it in order to avoid conflict. In a sense, they were unified that they could just get through the school year status quo, keep the peace, and that everyone would be better for it.

But is that true unity? Or is that a false sense of unity that is actually authoritative control mobilized by fear or ignorance that there could be something better?

How differently would history read if the Nazis rebelled against Hitler or if Christians stood up against the Crusades?

On the flip side, what would Christianity be like today if Luther had

For the One

recanted? What would the United States be like today if Lincoln gave in to political pressure? What would the universe be like today if Jesus submitted to the Pharisees?

Jesus Himself, the Lover and Uniter of humanity, often stood up and spoke out for what was right or needed to be reinterpreted, even though it caused problems in the "church" He was loyal to. So much so, they killed Him for it.

Yet Jesus Himself prayed for unity, for Oneness.

So there must be a different kind of oneness that He talked about than what we tend to think of—merely acquiescing to the majority, mere submission to persons of higher rank, mere agreement to avoid conflict. Like the kids on the bus ignoring the issues for fear of the consequences.

His prayer for unity

Let's look at Jesus' prayer:

> "I do not ask for these only, but also for those who will believe in me through their word, that they may all be one, . . . even as we are one, I in them and you in me, that they may become perfectly one, so that the world may know that you sent me and loved them even as you loved me" (John 17:20–23).

This prayer comes immediately after the Last Supper and before His arrest. Judas had already left and the disciples were puzzled by the things Jesus was saying to them, and He prayed this prayer to the Father out loud in front of the disciples.

There are three main parts—prayer for Himself, prayer for His disciples, prayer for all future believers—but let's focus on the prayer for future believers, His prayer for us.

There is a clear purpose: That they may be one.

The nature of the oneness: As the Father and Son are one.

Result of this oneness: That the world may believe that the Father sent the Son and loved us as He loves the Son.

That they may be one.

Jesus in Our Theology

What is One?

Though it seems to be the simplest of terms and numbers to understand, it is actually quite difficult mathematically. The definition of the number 1 is the foundation for all other math. In a recent TED talk called, "One is one . . . or is it?"[1] the presenter described how the number 1 is actually determined by what is defined as a whole unit. Thus, an apple, a whole bag of apples, or even an apple slice can be counted as 1. But, obviously these are not all the same thing. The reason for this is that these different units can be either composed meaning several whole things lumped together to make a larger thing such as a bag of apples, a married couple or an orchestra. Or these units can be partitioned, meaning a whole thing divided to make smaller things—for example, an apple slice or a pizza slice.

The TED talk goes on to share that once a unit has been either partitioned or composed, it is now considered a new whole unit that can be further composed or partitioned. It seems oneness can always be added to or taken from.

So the basic math we were taught in kindergarten—1+1=2 where 1=1—is not always correct. The number 1 always depends on what is considered the unit structure. Thus, the number 1 may represent many things or 1 seemingly single, or parts of what used to be a whole thing, but really 1 = all of the above, all at the same time.

> Though it seems to be the simplest of terms and numbers to understand, it is actually quite difficult mathematically.

In light of this, I'd like to introduce a new mathematical paradigm: 12 x 12,000 = 1.

Like the apple, different slices may be of different shapes and sizes, but they all share the same core. What is our core? What holds us together and remains our center once we are apart? What makes us One?

True unity

In *Seventh-day Adventists Believe*, there is a powerful image of unity: "Like the hub and spokes of a wheel, the closer church members (spokes)

For the One

come to Christ (the hub), the closer they come to each other."[2] Quoting Ellen White from *The Adventist Home*, this description continues, "The secret of true unity in the church and in the family is not diplomacy, not management, not a super-human effort to overcome difficulties—though there will be much of this to do—but Union with Christ."[3]

Let's look back at the nature of this oneness described by Jesus: As the Father and Son are one—" just as you, Father, are in me, and I in you, that they also may be in us."

The word "in" in the Greek is much more beautiful than our boring English translation. In the Jewish New Testament, it shares that, more than a geographical term, it was also used to get across a notion of deep mutual concern, "revealing the Father and the Son to be intimately involved and concerned with each other's existence."

The prayer in verses 1–5 gives us more context for this. Jesus prays that He would glorify God in what He is about to endure so all who believe may have eternal life. In verse 3, Jesus gives a definition of eternal life: To *know* God and Jesus whom God sent. This is important because the word here echoes that used in Hebrew for a husband and wife *knowing* each other and the oneness designed in Eden. It is a very relational and intimate knowledge like we read in the prayer for unity—"I in them and them in me."

The concept of this kind of knowing of God was missing in practice from the Jews—and perhaps many of us today. This is a significant and necessary factor as to whether we are one in Him or not. It is the idea of Intellect-versus-Relationship with both Jesus and each other. The Jewish "church" had one and lacked the other, resulting in the death of the One they supposedly worshipped.

The lack of intimate knowledge and relationship with God led to a superficial understanding of who He is. Scriptural knowledge alone often leads to misinterpretation and wrong application of the intellectual knowledge. Hence, most did not understand Jesus' sayings though they were "true." Spiritual things are spiritually discerned.

The unity Jesus prayed for cannot be merely an intellectual or theological agreement. It is much deeper and more personal than that. Like our relationships with our spouses aren't based on facts about a person, but on an experience of *knowing* each other. In His prayer for unity, Jesus likened it to His relating to His Father. Thus partaking in this oneness means we are entering into a relationship as a family unit. And, as in each family unit, it is composed of very different individuals. For example, my husband and I are one, but we are very different and definitely do not always agree.

Some are born into it and some are taken in—adopted—as orphans. But 12 x 12,000 = 1.

A prayer fulfilled

The second section of the John 17 prayer goes further into this dynamic. In verse 11, Jesus prays, "Holy Father, keep them [referring to the disciples] in your name, which you have given me, that they may be one, even as we are one."

Jesus did not pray for them to be the same. Nor did He create them the same! We all know and have read about how the disciples were definitely not unified—apart from Christ, their core. There were lots of natural tensions in the original 12: Simon the Zealot was pledged against people like Matthew the Publican; James and John claiming the right- and left-hand sides of Jesus in heaven caused jealousy among the others; earlier in the evening of this very prayer was the "Who is the greatest?" conversation.

> Some are born into it and some are taken in—adopted—as orphans. But 12 x 12,000 = 1.

But Jesus is what unified them. During His trial and death, they did just what He said they would do. They scattered—but He reunited them in His resurrection.

We see the fulfillment of Jesus' prayer for them to be one in Acts 2 at Pentecost, when they were all in one accord and the Spirit came upon them. Suddenly, their differences became their strengths as God used some to reach the Jews and others to reach the Gentiles, as they spoke in different tongues to reach different people. It was a movement of the Spirit working through diversity to glorify God and bring the world to Him.

Jesus prayed for a kind of unity that embraced diversity, but this is generally not an easy thing to do. Most of us tend to view people who are different from us or who have different views as enemies to our ordered way of thinking and living.

Valuing dissent

An article from the *Journal of Business Ethics* discusses two different types of dissent—"Principled Dissent" compared with "Malcontent Dissent."[4] The Malcontent Dissenter is one that seeks to divide and tear down an organization through negativity and an invitation to chaos. On the other hand, the Principled Dissenter is highly ethically motivated because their love for the organization and moral conscience will not allow them to be silent.

These dissenters are people who seek to make the organization better by standing for needed change. They want the organization to become more solid on its foundational principles and help with checks and balances necessary to avoid the corruption of natural institutional dangers including a "bureaucratic ethic" that prizes conformity with organizational ideals and ideologies, acquiescence to bosses, and avoiding blame. We see this even in our own history as union conferences were formed, partly to decentralize the power of the General Conference as disunity was forming due to its "kingly power."

The article goes on to say that if bureaucratic leadership continues, these organizations and its leadership end up full of like-minded people. A general policy of dishonesty and faking tends to govern everything. "Niceness" takes the place of genuine relationship, with the belief that social harmony and a lack of conflict are positive ways of accommodating and adjusting to people. They have become smiling faces, devoid of individual substance and integrity.

The alternative to this kind of superficially unified structure is recognizing principled dissent as different from other forms of criticism and opposition, and allowing the dissenter to be an important organizational voice. Principled dissent has the opportunity to bring humanity back into organizations. In Quaker communities, this type of dissent is encouraged as a means to cause further deliberations to protect and search for truth. It is considered a value, not a threat. Our goal for those with different ideas and opinions should not be mutual toleration but mutual comprehension that we may seek to truly understand each other's viewpoints and become mature as the body of Christ.

Ephesians 4:4–6 says we are baptized into one body with diverse gifts for the purpose of building up the church, the composed body of Christ. So why do we try to separate, dismember or partition ourselves from those who are different from us when together we can achieve brilliance?

Jesus was a loyal Jew who challenged the Jewish institution. His goal was never to divide the "church" but to save it! The Jewish community did not recognize this because they had lost their focus on the core of their beliefs, which was the Lamb of God who was present in their midst. They were so caught up in being and doing right, and fighting against anyone who disagreed with them, that they killed the One who was the foundation of their beliefs.

True unity

Which takes us to the true test of our unity and its result: "The world may know that you sent me and loved them even as you loved me" (John 17:23).

This is difficult because unity is hard to see. The life of Jesus in the Body of Christ is invisible. How are people to know of its existence and believe in Jesus? But the text gives us the answer—the unity in the church is made visible when we love one another. He calls for us to baptize every nation, every kindred, every tongue. He does not call us to be the same. Unity is not as much about whether we agree but how we disagree.

> Jesus was a loyal Jew who challenged the Jewish institution. His goal was never to divide the "church" but to save it!

The unity Jesus prayed for was a request from the Father, something to be given, not something manufactured. It is a gift from God by His Spirit, but just because it is a gift does not mean we are to be passive. We need to be active in bridging the gap between like and dislike, liberals and conservatives, those for women's ordination and those against, carnivores and vegetarians. We do not need to agree or even function in the same way, but we need to prayerfully take hold of each other's hands and seek to know each other on deeper levels than church politics or lifestyle choices, seeking instead to see God at work in each individual and let perfect love do its work

In a world starving for meaningful relationships, a supernaturally unified community of diverse people draws others to believe that Jesus is alive and within us. Love draws, but it must be true love, not superficial bureaucratic church "niceness." Love is not mere sentiment. It is not something used to disguise dislike. Romans 12:9 urges us to "let love be genuine" or "unfeigned." It goes beyond just those we are comfortable with. There is mutual contribution, giving and receiving. A recognized need of each other, of everyone as a part of the whole family unit. But this kind of love only comes from God.

In John 17:23, Jesus prays "that we may be brought into complete unity" or "that we may become perfect" depending on translation. Either way, the word here for perfect or complete is *"teleo"* which is the last word Jesus uttered on the cross: "It is finished" or complete, made perfect, made whole. True church unity takes place at the cross where we are all humbly submitted to One God and in need of One Savior, and where we are intimately concerned with each other's journey to get there. Oneness is meant to be a sharing of life. Like a mother and a baby who share an umbilical cord, we share a lifeline, not because we share ideas and opinions or just want to keep the "peace." Rather it is about to Whom we go to for sustained existence and strength for life.

The team dynamic

I used to be a nurse in a Pediatric ICU and I will never forget the first time I had to code someone. It was my patient—a two year old who had swallowed a tack. His lungs were filling with blood and he was dying.

I had some issues with some people I was working with that night. The respiratory therapist was making inappropriate comments to me. I was a new nurse graduate and the doctor did not trust or respect me yet. One of the nurses did not like me because I was a Christian who didn't drink and party. We had quite a few differences and underlying issues.

But when that child's heart stopped beating and his lungs stopped breathing, none of that mattered. Now we worked side by side, unified by a mission to save this child's life. The doctor was very patient with me as she gave the orders of what meds to give and what to do next. The therapists appropriately aided me in my compressions and life-giving breaths. The other nurse made encouraging comments and acted as my supporter throughout the process. Other nurses rallied to hold the mother as she screamed for her child to come back to life.

Suddenly the other issues became insignificant as we worked together to save this child's life. And afterward we all had more love and respect for each other that overshadowed the differences we had before.

We need to be united in what or who we are "for," not in what we are against. Our enemy is defeated and will soon cease to exist, but we will remain united in Christ, our core, for eternity.

Now, at the end of the greatest conflict in the history of the universe, we need to be One to save people from more than a swallowed tack, but from eternal death by lifting up Christ and making Him the center of all we say and do. Together, we stand for what He stood for, and pray for the presence and filling of the Holy Spirit to keep us a composed body of Christ. To be truly One with Jesus and the Father.

This will leave us with some different answers to "What is One?" In the mathematics of Revelation, 12 x 12,000 = 1.

So you tell me—or better yet, *show* me—what is One?

> We need to be united in what or who we are "for," not in what we are against.

---

1. Christopher Danielson, "One is one . . . or is it?" <http://ed.ted.com/lessons/one-is-one-or-is-it>.

2. General Conference of Seventh-day Adventists, *Seventh-day Adventists Believe: An exposition of the fundamental beliefs of the Seventh-day Adventist Church* (2nd edition), Pacific Press, 2005, page 206.

3. Ellen White, *The Adventist Home*, page 179.

4. Nasrin Shahinpoor and Bernard F Matt, "The Power of One: Dissent and Organizational Life," *Journal of Business Ethics*, Vol 74 No 1, 2007, pages 37–48.

"A quarterback and a coach went up to the temple to pray..."

Karl Haffner

Whether you paint your face and go shirtless to every game of your favorite (American) football team or if you could care less, you probably know about two of the more-talked-about names surrounding the sport.

The first is Tim Tebow. When he took over as quarterback of the ailing Denver Broncos, suddenly they started winning. It wasn't just the wins; it was how they were winning. Week after week, Tebow orchestrated these impossible, last-second, come-from-behind dramatic miracles. Statisticians have crunched the numbers and figured the odds of anybody pulling off what Tebow did are about 1 in 27 million! No wonder he is dubbed "The Miracle Man."

The nickname also refers to the fact that Tim Tebow is an outspoken, devout Christian. In fact, his name has become synonymous with praying. In American vernacular today, "Tebowing" means "praying."

Sports Illustrated columnist, Rick Reilly, figured nobody could be that squeaky clean, so he tried to dig up some dirt on Tebow. Instead of exposing a scandal, however, he learned things about Tebow that the

Jesus in Our Theology

public didn't know. Reilly tells of Tebow's ritual before every game:

> Tebow picks out someone who is suffering, or who is dying, or who is injured. He flies these people and their families to the game, rents them a car, puts them up in a nice hotel, buys them dinner (usually at a Dave & Buster's), gets them and their families pregame passes, visits with them just before kickoff (!), gets them 30-yard-line tickets down low, visits with them after the game (sometimes for an hour), has them walk him to his car, and sends them off with a basket of gifts. Home or road, win or lose, hero or goat.[1]

How can you not love this guy? Everyone loves Tim Tebow. In the height of his popularity, I would often regale the family with the latest Tebow story at our dinner table.

- "I heard on the news today that Tim Tebow is raising more than a million dollars to build a children's hospital."
- "Did you know that Tim Tebow has publicly pledged to keep himself pure until he gets married?"
- "Tebow was born to missionary parents in the Philippines. And he was home-schooled."

Almost every night I had a new story. As far as role models go, I am thankful for Tim Tebow. I can't think of a better professional athlete for my kid to emulate. So as you read the rest of this chapter, please keep this in mind: I am Tim Tebow's biggest fan.

The other name that has hogged the football headlines is Jerry Sandusky. He is the former assistant coach at Penn State University who was found guilty on 45 of the 48 charges of molestation of boys. I still remember when the story broke. Just seeing his face triggered a visceral impulse to throw a lamp at the TV. Nothing raises my ire more than accounts of grown men abusing boys for their own prurient pleasure. I understand why many people say, "Jerry Sandusky is a scumbag. I hate that man."

Two more men

Now keep those two men in mind as we consider the story of two more men. The parable is found in Luke 18:9-14.

First, notice to whom Jesus was speaking: "To some who were

For the One

confident of their own righteousness and looked down on everyone else" (Luke 18:9, NIV). Luke states two attributes: (1) self-righteous; and (2) condescending toward others.

Now when it comes to being self-righteous and having a condescending and judgmental spirit, we are dealing with a problem that is really hard to self-diagnose. For 25 years I have seen a steady stream of people parade through my office and confess sins that are so destructive. "Pastor," someone says, "You got to help me with my mismanaged anger because it's destroying my family." Or "Pastor, my eating disorder is killing me. Help!" Or "Pastor, my compulsive pornography addiction is undermining my marriage."

But I have never had anyone say, "Pastor, you got to help me with my spiritual conceit. I am so quick to condemn people. I am self-righteous and judgmental and condescending toward others. Please help me! My spiritual arrogance is sabotaging my soul and destroying my relationship with God." This sin is fatal—but we don't see it in ourselves. There is no 12-step program for the spiritually smug.

So to crack this mask of self-sufficiency, "Jesus told this parable: 'Two men went up to the temple to pray, one a Pharisee and the other a tax collector'" (Luke 18:9, 10, NIV).

The Pharisee

First, we are introduced to the Pharisee. "The Pharisee stood by himself and prayed: 'God, I thank you that I am not like other people—robbers, evildoers, adulterers—or even like this tax collector. I fast twice a week and give a tenth of all I get'" (Luke 19:11, 12, NIV).

Have you ever heard somebody praying, presumably to God, but it's obvious that they are really talking to someone within earshot? "God forgive my husband (who is listening right now) for selfishly forgetting our anniversary and tell Him that all things are forgiven if he were to pick up that gift for me that You know is on layaway right now at Macy's."

Frank Schaeffer, the son of Francis and Edith Schaeffer, founders of the fundamentalist community L'Abri in Switzerland, has written a memoir titled *Crazy for God: How I Grew Up as One of the Elect, Helped Found the Religious Right, and Lived to Take All (or Almost All) of It Back*.

Jesus in Our Theology

As the title suggests, Frank is quite cynical about matters of faith. In the book, he describes his mother's prayers. He writes:

> Sometimes Mom would hold forth in prayer for literally [hours] . . . When prayed out loud, the prayers were often not-so-subtle vehicles for sermons. These sermons, masquerading as prayers, were for the good of those here on earth who were eavesdropping on what was purporting to be a conversation with God but was really a way to say things to Dad that Mom didn't dare say out loud or a way for Dad or Mom to preach to an unbeliever. Praying out loud was also a way of advancing one's case—the advantage being that no one dared interrupt you or argue back. . . . I sometimes wondered if God tried to duck out of the room when He saw Mom coming.[2]

Likewise, I wonder if God tried to duck out of the temple when He saw this Pharisee coming to the temple. The Pharisee is not praying to God at all. He's broadcasting his goodness. The prayer is an unmasked recital of his righteousness.

He is so judgmental, this man. Good thing we're not that way, right? Or at least we're a lot more discreet and refined in our judgmental barbs.

> **The Pharisee is not praying to God at all. He's broadcasting his goodness.**

The other day I hit the drive-thru at Taco Bell and ordered a couple tacos (beans instead of beef, in case you are judging me). Only after I placed my order did I see the newest menu item—the Cantina Burrito. Only heaven knows why I fall for any "new" menu item at Taco Bell because, let's face it, every thing they serve at Taco Bell contains the same ingredients. Instead of putting the cheese on the beans, they come out with a "revolutionary new burrito" by putting beans on the cheese and then they charge an extra buck for the innovation. So don't ask me why I fell for their marketing scam, but I did. I yelled at the speaker: "Can I change my order? Make that one taco and I'll try your new Veggie Cantina Burrito."

The guy said, "OK, no problem." But then he left his transmitter on

For the One

so I could hear the ensuing dialogue with the girl preparing the food. This gave me the opportunity to exercise my primary spiritual gift—eavesdropping. And since I'm using this story in a book, I think my taco qualifies as a tax deduction!

So when the guy told this girl to change my order, she was incredulous. "He changed his order? What an idiot! Why did you let the idiot change his order?"

The guy defended me. "Don't judge him," he said. "Your job is not to judge. Your job is to make burritos."

Again, she reiterated, "The guy is an idiot."

Then he said something you don't expect to hear at a drive-thru. "Don't judge the guy," he said firmly. "Only God can judge."

That'll preach! I thought. *"Only God can judge."*

Imagine if our churches modeled this kind of non-judgmental love. Our Lady of Lourdes Catholic Church in Daytona, Florida, attempts to live out this expression of non-judgmental love. In their bulletin they publish this welcome to visitors:

> We extend a special welcome to those who are single, married, divorced, gay, filthy rich, dirt poor, *yo no habla Ingles*. We extend a special welcome to those who are crying newborns, skinny as a rail or could afford to lose a few pounds. We welcome you if you can sing like Andrea Bocelli or like our pastor who can't carry a note in a bucket. You're welcome here if you're "just browsing," just woke up or just got out of jail. We don't care if you're more Catholic than the Pope, or haven't been in church since little Joey's baptism.
>
> We extend a special welcome to those who are over 60 but not grown up yet, and to teenagers who are growing up too fast. We welcome soccer moms, NASCAR dads, starving artists, tree-huggers, latte-sippers, vegetarians, junk-food eaters. We welcome those who are in recovery or still addicted. We welcome you if you're having problems or you're down in the dumps or if you don't like "organized religion," we've been there too.
>
> If you blew all your offering money at the dog track, you're welcome here. We offer a special welcome to those who

think the earth is flat, work too hard, don't work, can't spell, or because grandma is in town and wanted to go to church.

We welcome those who are inked, pierced or both. We offer a special welcome to those who could use a prayer right now, had religion shoved down your throat as a kid or got lost in traffic and wound up here by mistake. We welcome tourists, seekers and doubters, bleeding hearts . . . and you![3]

Imagine if our churches threw down a welcome mat like that. I suspect people would be trampling over each other to get in. Instead, I fear that this Pharisee's attitude is more the norm. We're thankful that our churches are safe harbors from "the bad guys."

The Pharisee continues his prayer, informing God, "I fast twice a week" (Luke 18:12, NIV). His claims are quite loaded. Everyone listening to Jesus would have noted the man's righteousness. According to Leviticus 25, an Israelite was only required by the law to fast once a year during the Day of Atonement. This guy fasts twice a week—100 times more than what the law requires.

Then he says, "I give a tenth of *all* I get" (Luke 18:12, NIV, italics mine). Don't skim over the small word "all." According to Old Testament law, farmers would have already tithed on commodities like wine, grain or oil. So it wasn't necessary to pay an additional tithe on such items. But this guy goes ahead and tithes on everything—above and beyond the minimum required.

> We're thankful that our churches are safe harbors from "the bad guys."

Other items did not require a tithe. For example, one rabbinic teaching said this: "You are not required to tithe on celery." I ask you: Of what value is celery? Why do we even bother with the stalk? It's not a real food like M&Ms or Fig Newtons or gluten burgers. Apparently God doesn't like celery either!

So this Pharisee is doing serious extra-credit work. He assumes that he can enhance his status in the eyes of God by all of his religious activities. This man is so blind that he doesn't even see how obnoxiously self-absorbed he is. He prays to God, but really it's just a recitation of his works, his devotion, and his righteousness. "Me, me, me"—that's the tenor of his prayer.

Ever met somebody like that? Some time ago my wife and I went to lunch with a church administrator from another state. The whole meal he kept name-dropping. "I'm friends with this church leader, and I know so and so, and me, I, me, mine, myself, I'm . . ." It was suffocating. The most painful part was how clueless he was to his narcissistic air.

On our drive home, I said to Cherié, "It was nauseating how controlling and careful he was to make the conversation only about him." Then I had this unsettling thought and I asked her, "Do I ever do that?"

Silence.

"Well," she finally said, "you may want to talk to a trusted friend about that."

So I did. The next week, I was having lunch with Oprah . . .

Not really! I just made that whole story up. But should the ugly truth get told, the tale is based on a true story. The Pharisee's cancer of spiritual narcissism poisons my soul too. No doubt, the disease is way more pervasive than I even know.

Now it's critical to understand that at this point in the story everybody listening in Jesus' day would have felt very favorable toward the Pharisee. Since we already know the punch line and we know of the larger body of work with respect to the Pharisees, we do not naturally side with the religious guy. We are repulsed by his arrogance and self-righteousness—not so, when Jesus told the story.

Back then everybody would have venerated the Pharisee. He was holy. Generous. Committed. The listeners did not scorn him nor find him repulsive. He was the Tim Tebow of their day. In our day, we are not offended by Tebow's generous life—nor should we be. He is a great man of God.

The tax collector

Enter the tax collector. He was the Jerry Sandusky of the day. Nobody felt fuzzy, warm feelings toward this guy. The mere mention of his name would have triggered an indignant outrage from the crowd.

Jesus in Our Theology

No rabbi in the ancient world—other than Jesus—ever told a story that featured a tax collector as the hero. Just his name knotted stomachs and wrinkled foreheads, pointed fingers and hurried heartbeats.

Jesus continued, "But the tax collector stood at a distance. He would not even look up to heaven, but beat his breast and said, 'God, have mercy on me, a sinner'" (Luke 18:13, NIV).

The text says that both men separated themselves—but for very different reasons. The tax collector "beat his breast." The act of beating one's chest was considered an expression of extreme agony in that culture; it was very rare. This gesture is only mentioned twice in scripture—once here and the other time when Jesus is crucified at Golgotha.

Listen to his simple prayer: "God have mercy on me, a sinner." There is no long list of good deeds here. It is short, stark and dark.

The tax collector understands his utter and absolute spiritual depravity. He has no delusion that he deserves anything from a just and holy God. Absent are any claims of piety. Silenced are any boasts of godly bravado. There is no hint of entitlement in his prayer.

> My judgmental, jaded heart is worse than whatever sin I see in others—and I don't even know it.

Making it personal

So is there any Pharisee heresy in your heart? Do you feel a tinge of pleasure when you're the first to hear about the head elder's arrest for drunk driving (assuming you're not the head elder)? Ever find yourself scowling in judgment against the single mom who can't control her kids in church? Any scent of spiritual smugness when the pastor gets busted for sleeping in the wrong bed?

What's scary to me is how firmly lodged this Pharisee is in me and I don't even see him. He enjoys a long-term lease and I can't even admit that he lives in my neighborhood. My judgmental, jaded heart is worse than whatever sin I see in others—and I don't even know it. I have such a corrupt heart. This is what Jesus was trying to expose in His story.

Jeremiah 17:9 (NKJV) says it well: "The heart is deceitful above all

For the One

things, And desperately wicked; Who can know it?" We see the evil in others with blinding clarity while we are clearly blind to the evil polluting our own hearts.

The very best acts of righteousness performed by the Pharisee or Tim Tebow or you or me—the best we can offer amounts to a mountain of used rags. The very best works that we can offer flow out of such corrupt hearts with selfish, insidious, dark, and twisted motives.

The best you got is garbage. You can be impeccably orthodox and doctrinally pure, right down to your decaffeinated, non-alcoholic, smoke-free, vegan, home-schooled little soul, but you're no less a wretched sinner in need of God's grace.

Somehow, I'm tempted to think that because I've never molested a kid or murdered an enemy or cheated on my wife, my sins aren't so bad. So I'm inclined to believe that God's getting a good deal with me—like when God paid it all on Calvary for me, He got a refund. Surely God's impressed with my commitment, isn't He? After all, I'm a card-carrying ASI, GYC, NAD, SDA.

God have M-E-R-C-Y.

Here's the inconvenient reality of grace: God loves Jerry Sandusky every bit as much as He loves Tim Tebow. There is nothing that Tim Tebow has done that has earned him favor in God's sight; and there is nothing that Jerry Sandusky has done that has disqualified him from heaven. It's not fair. And it's terribly unsettling. But it's true. And it's grace.

Jerry Bridges put it this way: "Your worst days are never so bad that you are beyond the reach of God's grace. And your best days are never so good that you are beyond the need of God's grace."[4] Put another way: "Your Sandusky days are never so bad that you are beyond the *reach* of God's grace. And your Tebow days are never so good that you are beyond the *need* of God's grace."

The good news in all of this is that God can even love a hardened self-righteous, judgmental, elder-brother Pharisee like me. Jesus says, "Those whom I love I rebuke and discipline" (Revelation 3:19, NIV). That sounds strange at first and yet when Jesus rebukes and chastens He has tears in His voice.

In Matthew 23, we find one of the most hard-hitting chapters in all

Jesus' experience. Study the whole chapter and you will see that Jesus uses words such as "You scribes and Pharisees, hypocrites, you blind guides, you fool and blind," again, "you blind guides." Once more, "Hypocrites, ye snakes and sons of snakes."

Now how in the world can you have tears in your voice and say those words? I do not know. Gravel in my throat as I bark such words? Sure. But tears? Not hardly. And yet that's what Jesus had. For He promised that if anyone opens the door, He will come in and a friendship will flourish. What a beautiful invitation from the One who rebukes and chastens because He loves.

Here's the bottom line: Jesus loves bank robbers. And Jesuits. And traffickers. And teachers. And athletes. And Muslims. And even Pharisees. All of us are beloved sinners. All of us are cherished children. All of us are in need of God's grace.

Again, the story

So here's our story one more time:

> To priests and rabbis and pastors and vegans and Sabbathkeepers and Republicans who picket abortion clinics and rail on homosexuals, a wise teacher told this story: "Two men went up to Notre Dame Cathedral to pray, one a committed Christian quarterback who was worshiped around the world for his good deeds; and the other man, a coach, a known paedophile. The quarterback stood by the altar and prayed: 'God, I thank you that you can use me to build churches and schools and hospitals and orphanages around the world. Thank you, God, for using me to star in a pro-life commercial during the Super Bowl. I thank you, Oh God, for the public platform upon which I pray and witness to millions. Thank you for the privilege of sharing your love to the terminally ill before games. I gladly surrender my substantial tithe to your cause. Grant me strength to fast and pray and serve you. Amen.'

> What a beautiful invitation from the One who rebukes and chastens because He loves.

For the One

"But the coach stood at a distance. He would not even look up to heaven, but succumbed to long, jagged sobs in a fetal position on the floor. 'Oh my God. Oh God, God,' he labored, 'have mercy on me. There is no human being less deserving and more despicable than me. For my appalling acts of cruelty to kids, I deserve to be tortured and crucified. God, have mercy on me.'

"I tell you the truth," said the wise teacher, "this coach, rather than the quarterback, went home justified before God. For all those who exalt themselves will be humbled, and those who humble themselves will be exalted. Let she, let he, who has ears to hear, let them hear what the Spirit says. Amen."

---

1. Rick Reilly, "I believe in Tim Tebow," <espn.go.com/espn/story/_/id/7455943/believing-tim-tebow>.

2. Frank Schaeffer, *Crazy for God: How I Grew Up as One of the Elect, Helped Found the Religious Right, and Lived to Take All (or Almost All) of It Back*, De Capo Press, 2008, Chapter 25.

3. <www.jonacuff.com/stuffchristianslike/2012/07/how-to-welcome-people-to-your-church>.

4. Jerry Bridges, *Holiness day by day: Transformational Thoughts for Your Spiritual Journey*, NavPress, 2008, Kindle file.

Jesus. Wow.

Recognizing Jesus as Lord

Stephan Sigg

Years ago, my Homiletics teacher told me that any preacher should be able to express the central thought of his or her sermon in one single sentence. I always had difficulties with that kind of exercise. But The One Project has helped me.

The essential message in one sentence or even two words: Just Jesus!

When I was asked to reflect on Jesus as portrayed in one of the gospels, my first thought was that Mark is perfect for The One Project. Mark similarly expressed the essential message of his gospel in a few words. Mark 1:1: "Beginning of the Good News of Jesus the Christ, the Son of God." Period.

With one sentence, Mark boils down his whole writing to its essence. Many interpreters understand Mark's beginning to be some kind of a headline. I rather see it as the central Christian confession followed by a large appendix—the rest of his book.

Beginning with his first word—*arché*—Mark connects the Story of Salvation with the Story of Creation. Here is something new happening, something incredible and huge: Jesus, the Messiah. It is the Beginning of the Gospel—the Good News—and there is no ending to that. If you go through the book of Mark, you will finally discover that Mark finishes his writing with the notion that the Gospel continues—Jesus working through His disciples, up to this day.

With and in Jesus, the gospel begins and unfolds, but it doesn't end. The story of salvation is a serial story because, in Jesus, there is

For the One

no ending to the Good News. And by believing, trusting in Jesus, we become part of it. Our story of salvation begins in Jesus.

Our salvation in Jesus is not merely a historical incident, an act on the cross, but a state of being with an everlasting perspective. Our salvation begins in embracing Jesus as our Lord and it stands in Him for an everlasting life. Jesus is our gospel forever. Mark's confession is Jesus, the Christ, the Anointed, the Son of God. The Lord of life. Jesus. All.

What a wonderful opening of the Gospel of Mark. And I could stop here. The essential has been said.

However, I was asked to reflect on Jesus in the gospel not on Jesus, the Gospel. So in my excitement about the Good News of the great Christian confession that Jesus is the Messiah, the Son of God, that He is Lord, I was struck by the fact that this excitement has not been shared by Jesus' own people.

The ordinary messiah

> He went away from there and came to his hometown, and his disciples followed him. And on the Sabbath he began to teach in the synagogue, and many who heard him were astonished, saying, "Where did this man get these things? What is the wisdom given to him? How are such mighty works done by his hands? Is not this the carpenter, the son of Mary and brother of James and Joses and Judas and Simon? And are not his sisters here with us?" And they took offense at him. And Jesus said to them, "A prophet is not without honor, except in his hometown and among his relatives and in his own household." And he could do no mighty work there, except that he laid his hands on a few sick people and healed them (Mark 6:1–5).

Nazareth was home for Jesus. It was where He had grown up, where He had played in the streets with other children, where He went to worship on Sabbath. Childhood memories at every corner.

These were His people. And now He was back in His hometown. He was already well known in the whole country, but nowhere better than there. And on Sabbath, Jesus taught in the synagogue, probably not for the first time. Probably Jesus has already impressed His people

Jesus in Our Theology

on several occasions. If someone had amazed the scholars of Jerusalem at the age of 12 (see Luke 2:46, 47), He must have amazed others at home as well.

But not this time. After the preaching, they were taken aback, despite the fact that they saw the wisdom and Jesus' mighty works. In Israel, it was known that wisdom and power are attributes of God—and the coming Messiah (see Job 11:2). So somehow the people of Nazareth associate Jesus with the central attributes of the expected Messiah—but this only raised more questions. "Where does this man have all this from? We do know him! Here with us, that's where he has grown up, here, just like all his siblings."

This was a group of people who knew Jesus better than anyone else. They had been around with Jesus all His life. They acknowledged His wisdom and power over evil spirits, diseases, the forces of nature and even death. But instead of being excited, they were offended.

In Nazareth, Jesus was reduced to His earthly origins and squeezed into His family frame. The people recognize Jesus not as Lord but only as a "*Tekton*," a carpenter and the son of Mary. That is the pigeonhole they have for Jesus. That is where he has to fit in. They stopped at the human nature of Jesus. Their offense reveals that, ultimately, they had problems with the concept of incarnation.

> In Nazareth, Jesus was reduced to His earthly origins and squeezed into His family frame.

How can Jesus be the Messiah when he is one of us? Grown up in an ordinary town? Totally human? Part of our culture, sharing our everyday life?

Their concept of the Messiah and His holiness excluded everyday life: work, play, family, eating, laughing, celebrating. Jesus shared all this with us. But somehow this "Messiah" was not holy enough. Jesus did not meet their expectations of the Son of God and heavenly King.

Interestingly, there are always people in church who somehow claim to know Jesus better. They claim to know exactly how He is, what He thinks, what He likes or how He feels. There are many pigeonholes for Jesus, even very "religious" ones.

In His home "church," Jesus became a stranger, precisely because He seemed so well known. They acknowledged somehow Jesus' wisdom and power, but they didn't entrust themselves to it.

In His hometown, Jesus was *tekton*, not Lord. He was the son of Mary, but not the Son of God. There is no other place where the people know more about Jesus but exactly here among *His people* Jesus is reduced to being small and common. Walter Grundmann—a German interpreter—comments: "It is the familiarness with Him that prevents them from believing."[1]

The Messiah amazed

Jesus was amazed at their response—in Greek, *thaumazo*. He was puzzled about their lack of faith. Here, where they knew Him best, they make Him small. Familiarity with Jesus prevents them from believing, from surrendering, from truly acknowledging Jesus as Lord.

Jesus is puzzled: "These are my people. This is my 'church' on Sabbath!"

And I am disturbed: These were God's peculiar people, the descendants of Abraham, the covenant people. They had the temple. They knew the law. They had scripture. They even knew Jesus. But they were so self-confident, so consumed by their own religion and the truth as they knew it that finally they missed the Son of God, the Lord.

Interestingly, there is only one other story where Jesus is described with the word *thaumazo*. Although this means I have to step into the territory of another of the gospels, let's go there because the two incidents where Jesus is puzzled are interrelated and contrasting in a surprising way.

It's the story of the centurion in Capernaum, who was seeking healing for his servant (see Matthew 8:5–13). Jesus had chosen this small fishing village on the Sea of Galilee as his new home after having left Nazareth (see Matthew 4:13). Being a border location toward the north, Capernaum was also a base for mercenary soldiers serving Herod Antipas.

It is unlikely that the presence of soldiers who collaborated with Rome found great welcome. They were part of the occupying power openly detested by the inhabitants. Moreover, the mercenaries were unbelievers, uncircumcised and not of Abraham's descendants. They did not belong to the "church" and had no baptismal certificate.

It is precisely one of these men who was the main character of Jesus' second amazement. This was a centurion, an officer responsible for 100 soldiers, and to be a Roman centurion was considered the opposite of being a believer.

Jesus had just come home to Capernaum after one of His journeys, and the soldier stood before Jesus and asked Him to heal his servant, who was critically ill.

This was an unusual request. According to the Roman author Varro (who lived in the time of Jesus), the only difference between a slave and the cattle or a carriage was that the slave could speak. And the best you could do was to chase a sick slave away and buy a new one.

Our centurion obviously saw things differently. Underneath his iron armor, he had a compassionate heart. He did all he could to help his servant. And he turned to Jesus.

Somehow he must have heard about Him. Even more, the centurion must have been deeply touched by the teachings and doings of Jesus, by Jesus' wisdom and power. Instead of standing before Jesus with a wide stance or looking down demandingly from the high horse, he asked, rather than commanded. He met Jesus, aware of his own unworthiness. His is a totally different attitude toward Jesus than that of the people in Nazareth.

Here Jesus is "*Kyrie*"—the Master, the Lord! Twice, the centurion called Jesus that (see verses 6 and 8). This was remarkable. He even considered himself unworthy of Jesus entering his house. The Jewish Mishna taught that a pious Jew would become impure by entering a heathen's house (see also John 18:28). Our centurion seems to know this and his attitude reveals much more than mere acceptance of cultural customs. This commander bows before the Redeemer.

For the One

"One word of me and 100 seasoned soldiers march lock-step," he said to Jesus. "One sign of me and none of them will move or even bat an eyelid. And here I am, just a human being and as such subject to other human beings. But you are the Lord! All is subject to you. Just one word from You and my servant will be healed."

What humility and self-awareness in the presence of the Lord!

Jesus was puzzled—and astonished (*thaumazo*). The centurion was not only a caring person, interceding for a slave, disclosing his hopes for a miraculous healing, here was a man revealing his humble heart in faith in surrender to the Lordship of Jesus the Christ.

A heathen confessing Jesus to be Lord: Jesus was amazed. He had not found such faith among the people of Israel. His was a faith not spoiled by any kind of self-righteousness or religious superiority, a faith abandoning whatever claim or wanting to be in the right.

The positive astonishment of Jesus honoring this faith finally was accentuated by Jesus saying to the centurion, "Let it be done for you as you have believed" (verse 13).

The two stories

Two totally different stories: on one side, the people of Jesus' hometown—His "church"; on the other side, a Roman soldier.

Among His own people, Jesus is *tekton*. For the centurion, Jesus is *kyrie*. Here the centurion admitted his "smallness"; among His people, Jesus was made small, reduced to "Yeah, we know him, we can handle him."

One story is all about religious people knowing Jesus; the other about a heathen soldier surrendering to the Lord.

And Jesus is amazed. Twice. Here was lack of faith in His "church" and there was genuine faith in an unexpected place.

As we see these two experiences of Jesus, we might be amazed as well.

The first wow

Jesus found faith in an unexpected place, a faith he had not found in Israel and certainly not in Nazareth. Can there be genuine faith in Jesus outside of Israel? Among those who are not "us"?

Jesus in Our Theology

Or as the old Israel, can we be in danger of cultivating a religious culture of separation that we finally miss seeing and appreciating how the Holy Spirit is moving people in other places? Can it be that in all our concerns to secure Adventist orthodoxy, we could miss rooting our identity in Christ our Lord?

As foreshadowed in Nazareth, Israel's fate reminds us that it is possible that God's people end up being more into cultivating and preserving their own religion, orthodoxy, and peculiar identity than fostering genuine faith in Jesus the Lord. Israel is a constant reminder that the "We are" approach or the "We know" attitude is dangerous. As in Nazareth, we can have it all—even Jesus living among us—but still miss Christ. Jesus was amazed.

The second wow

Familiarity with Jesus can make Jesus small. You can know Jesus but miss the Lord. As a church, we have been there. The whole theological conflict in our Adventist church culminating in 1888 was about the fact that in the course of defending and upholding truth, holiness and obedience, we were in real danger of losing Christ. As Adventists, we were so familiar with Christ that we became "dry like the hills of Gilboa." He almost fell out of the Adventist picture—and this is still a danger.

> Familiarity with Jesus can make Jesus small. You can know Jesus but miss the Lord. As a church, we have been there.

After my two years of internship as a young Adventist pastor, a highly respected church member came to counsel me. "I hear you preaching Christ," he said. "Fine—but that is what all the other churches do as well. You should preach the Adventist message! What about Daniel and Revelation? What about the prophetic message about the end-time, the shaking, the judgment, the last generation and the final sealing? That is what we need to hear."

I have no problem with such teachings—as long as they are based on scripture and interpreted through the gospel of Christ. But there is a deep-rooted danger in our concern for "the truth" that we reduce

Jesus to just one paragraph of our fundamental beliefs. Jesus is not one among the 28 Adventist Fundamental Beliefs. Rather, He *is* the fundamental Adventist Belief through whom all other "beliefs" unfold and find their meaning.

This has to be evident in all our teaching and preaching. If not, we are in danger of making Jesus small and denying His Lordship. If we are not focused on Jesus—the One—the truth becomes powerless. In Nazareth, Jesus couldn't do much.

The third wow

Jesus said to the centurion, literally, "Go—and as you have believed, so be it to you." Jesus refers more to *how* the centurion believed than to *what* he believed. Can it be that the how we believe matters and not just what we believe, that genuine faith is more about an attitude of surrender to the Lordship of Christ with compassion and love, than acknowledging a system of beliefs as truth?

Now, I am far away from trying to play the one against the other. As a Jesus follower, I became an Adventist because of biblical doctrines. However, as careful students of the New Testament, we know that the ultimate goal of our faith is to love and live as Jesus did. The ultimate goal of all teachings, all truth, is genuine love from a pure heart, says the apostle Paul (see 1 Corinthians 13). Knowledge puffs up but love builds up.

In the parable of the sheep and the goats in Matthew 25, *how* people related to their neighbors becomes the determining factor for the separation of the righteous from the unrighteous. So when we talk about faith and surrendering to the Lordship of Jesus, is this more about what we believe or how we live it?

Amazing Jesus?

Jesus was amazed—twice. In Nazareth, among His own people, there was lack of faith in the context of religious pride and knowing it all. In Capernaum, there was genuine faith in the context of surrender, and true compassion and care for others.

What would you like to see Jesus be amazed about among us?

Jesus in Our Theology

Let's not stop celebrating the supremacy of Jesus, the Everlasting Gospel of the Christ, the Son of God, in our lives and church.

1. Walter Grundmann, *Das Evangelium nach Markus*, ThHK 2, Evangelische Verlagsanstalt, 1989, page 157.

A Second Touch
Re-discovering Jesus

Randy Roberts

The Adventist Christian world in which I was reared was steeped in morality. It isn't that people never let their hair down. I suspect most of us did—when no-one else was watching. But, as the storyteller Garrison Keillor once said, even when we let our hair down, not much happened, because our hair was pretty short.

On occasion someone would try to get serious about sinning. They seemed to take Tony Campolo's advice seriously: "If you're going to hell anyway, you may as well go with some degree of dignity!" But even when they got caught with their hand in the cookie jar, they usually had a handful of health-food cookies—and you know what *that's* like!

As I've gotten older and learned more about people, I now realize that signs of trouble were all around me, pervading the moral world in which I lived. But, back then, I couldn't have told you that. I just knew that life—religious life, *church* life, the *Christian* life—was about doing the right, the good, the *moral* things.

I suppose that's why when, while in college, I first heard a song by an Adventist songwriter named Brad McIntyre, I immediately related to it. The song was entitled, "The Adventist Blues."[1] Here are some of the words:

> Now I don't drink and I don't swear
> I don't take dope or have long hair
> I go to church each week, oh, yes I do.
>
> I never eat before going to bed,
> I'll drink a glass of juice instead,
> And I jog each day at least a mile or two.
>
> Now all my life I've been pretty good

Jesus in Our Theology

> I've always done just what I should
> My parents were missionaries overseas.
>
> I got all As in Bible class
> And studied hard so I could pass
> And even bought my books from the ABCs.

The song continues in the same vein—a vein to which I could distinctly relate. But when it came to the end, it asked a question that pulled me up short.

> Yes, I found the church where I belong,
> I don't think I've done anything wrong
> For at least two years—or maybe three.
>
> I know I'm walking in the light,
> Sometimes I'm bored, but that's all right,
> Because there's a crown in heaven just for me.
>
> But recently I've heard some talk,
> They say I need a closer walk
> With Jesus, if I'll only let Him in.
>
> Well, I'm all for that, I'll give it a try,
> Though I often wonder why
> And ask myself, just where does *He* fit in?

That song—and its ending question—haunted me. It left me feeling like there was something about this faith—something about Christianity, more specifically, something about Adventism—that I just wasn't getting. It seemed there was some key element missing, something I somehow couldn't see.

When everything changed

I suppose that missing piece provides the reason why I relate to what happens in the central part of the gospel of Mark. The Pharisees had just asked Jesus for a sign and Jesus had said, "You're not getting one." He then got into a boat with His disciples and crossed to the other side

For the One

of the lake. While they were on their way across, the disciples realized they had forgotten to bring sufficient bread to feed them all. While they were talking about that, Jesus said to them, "Be careful. Watch out for the yeast of the Pharisees and that of Herod" (see Mark 8:15). They tried to figure out what that meant and finally concluded that Jesus had noticed that they hadn't brought enough bread.

So Jesus—as close to frustration as you'll ever see Him—said to them, "Don't you get it?! Why are you talking about bread? Don't you understand? Don't you remember the 5000 I fed awhile back, or the 4000 I *just* fed?! *Can't you see?*"

He pressed on. "In fact, when I broke the five loaves for the 5000, how many baskets full of leftover pieces did you pick up?"

"Twelve," they said.

"And when I broke seven loaves for 4000, how many basketfuls did you pick up?"

"Seven."

And he asked again, "Do you *still* not understand? Having experienced *both* of those miracles, are you *still* worried about bread?! Are you serious?! Are you *blind*?!"

Right about then, some people came bringing a blind man to Jesus. "Can you please heal him?" Remember: Jesus' words—"Do you *still* not understand? Can you *still* not see? Are you *still* blind?"—are still hanging in the air.

Then comes what has to qualify as one of the most bizarre incidents in the life of Christ. Yet, for all its strangeness, scholars say that this story is at the heart of Mark's gospel. In fact, it's a turning point in Mark's gospel.

Eugene Peterson points out that, up to this point in Mark, this gospel has had a certain leisurely and meandering quality to it. Jesus, he says, doesn't seem to be going anywhere in particular. He drifts from village to village, goes off by Himself to pray, worships in the synagogues, goes home to eat with anyone who'll have Him, and goes boating with His friends on the lake. It isn't that He's aimless or lazy, because there's always energy and intensity. It's just that He seems to have all the time in the world.

But with this central passage, everything changed. After this, Jesus headed straight for Jerusalem. There's urgency, intensity, gravity. Three times in three successive chapters, He said, "I'm going to suffer, be killed and rise again." After this, there were no more miracles. The focus changed completely and was placed only on Calvary.

So this story in Mark 8:22–26 is the critical event—the bend in the road—in Mark's gospel.

A second-time miracle

Jesus took the blind man by the hand. "Come here," He said, and led him outside the village. He spat on the man's eyes.

"OK," Jesus said. "Read the top line on the chart."

"What chart?"

"On the wall."

"What wall?"

"Uh-oh," said Jesus. "We've got a problem. Can you see anything at all?"

"Well, I see people like trees walking. They're indistinct. Blurry. Hazy. Unclear."

"Well, that's not good enough." And He touched his eyes again. "Can you see now?"

"Wow!" the man exclaimed. "Yes! Yes! I see everything clearly now!"

What in the world was that all about?! Was Jesus having a bad day? We know the frame of mind He was in when this story began. He was . . . *I don't know the right word* . . . Discouraged? Bewildered? Frustrated? Despairing? His disciples just didn't get it; they couldn't see. And then came this man, wanting to be healed, and yet it took a two-step process to do it.

> This is the only time in any of the four gospels where a miracle required a second touch to be completed.

This is the only time in any of the four gospels where a miracle required a second touch to be completed. What was going on?

Putting it in context

As is so often the case, context is important. So by reading the next passage in Mark's gospel—Mark 8:27–29—we find some clues as to what Jesus was doing.

For the One

"Who do the people say that I am?" Jesus asked.

"Well, Jesus, they're not sure. They're confused. It isn't that they don't appreciate You or Your role or what You do. In fact, they think You're great! They think You're John the Baptist or Elijah or Jeremiah or one of the prophets!"

"So, they think I've come from God, do the work of God, speak the words of God, and do God's bidding. They're sure I'm great—but they're not sure who I am?"

"That's right, Jesus! They think You're great! But, who You are? Well, they're not so clear about that. When they try to see who You are, You're kind of indistinct. Blurry. Hazy. Unclear. You look like a tree, walking. And they wonder, 'Just where does He fit in?'"

"And what about you?" Jesus asked. "Who do you say that I am?"

And for all the times he stuck his foot in his mouth, Peter answered with stunning clarity on this occasion. "You are the Christ. The Messiah." In Matthew's gospel, Peter said, "You are the Christ, the Son of the living God" (Matthew 16:16).

Also in Matthew's gospel, Jesus responded to Peter, "Peter, flesh and blood did not reveal that to you. My Father in heaven did" (see Matthew 16:17). In other words, "You would never have arrived at that conclusion on your own. It came from divine inspiration."

Two pastors

Jesus' two questions echo down through time, all the way to us today. Two questions: *Can you see? Then who am I?* It's so tempting to say, "Well, Jesus is great! I mean, how can you match what He does?! He's the greatest! But, you see, we've got these other things that are great, too!" But to answer with the clarity of Peter, the clarity that says Jesus is "all"? Well, that's a little harder.

Can you see? Then who am I?

Over time, we have not answered those questions very well. I think, for example, of an incident that occurred on a key day in my life, my ordination to the gospel ministry. It illustrates so well the Jesus-fuzziness evident at times in our community of faith.

Anita and I were walking up to the auditorium where the ordination would take place. I was feeling excited, but on a deeper, more private level, I was keenly aware of my unworthiness for this high calling. Sure, I had grown up in a moral world. But I had been through times, in private, when I had been on a first-name basis with sin. So, walking toward my ordination, I was keenly aware of the twin feelings of the awesomeness of the task to which I had been called, and the recognition of my own inadequacies and lack of qualifications for the task.

An experienced pastor stopped me and asked, "Aren't you being ordained today?"

"Yes, sir, that's right."

"How do you feel?"

"Oh, well, you know, I'm very excited and very honored, but it's all kind of overwhelming. I don't deserve this."

"Well, let me give you a piece of advice," he said "something I learned years ago that might also help you in your ministerial career."

He proceeded to carefully show me how to wear a paper clip behind my tie. "I've learned that if you do that, no-one will criticize you for wearing a tie clasp, and yet you can still hold your tie in place."

Well, that left me cold.

We finished that conversation, walked a few more paces and another pastor stopped us, someone who had also been in pastoral ministry for many years.

"Are you being ordained today?"

"Yes, sir."

"How do you feel?"

"Well, not as good as I did a minute ago! I'm excited and honored—but a bit overwhelmed."

"Overwhelmed? How so?"

"Well, you know. This is an awesome calling. Who can deserve it? I certainly don't."

And he said, "You know what? You're right. You don't deserve it. In fact, the only reason you'll be up there today is because He called you, and He didn't call you because you merit it. But since He called you,

> "Let me give you a piece of advice," he said, "something I learned years ago that might also help you in your ministerial career."

For the One

He will qualify you. You stand there in His righteousness. Be grateful, because since He is worthy, you don't have to be."

I know the temptation is to disparage the first pastor. That's what I want to do. After all, you know what his attitude said. It simply said: "Jesus is great! He's wonderful! He's so important to what we're trying to do! But, let me tell you what's really exciting about ministry: paper clips! That's what's really exciting!"

We want to denigrate and deride him. But it strikes me—we wouldn't disparage a man who can't see clearly, would we? "What's wrong with you?! You can't read that letter on the top line of the chart? Get it together!"

So don't mock him. He just couldn't see very clearly. He needed the second touch of Jesus. That would open his eyes and allow him to finally see clearly who Jesus is and the centrality of His role in our lives. "You are the Christ, the Son of the living God!"

That second touch

Have you met a Seventh-day Adventist in need of the second touch of Jesus?

What about the young woman who's been around the block and down the hall, yet she comes to her pastor and says, "Pastor, I'm afraid God won't accept me"?

The pastor says, "Jesus says that the one who comes to Him He will never reject."

She says, "Oh, I wish . . . I just *wish* I could believe that!"

And the pastor says, "What you really need is the second touch of the Jesus, so you can see clearly that Jesus does His best work with broken people."

Have you met a Seventh-day Adventist in need of the second touch of Jesus?

What about the Adventist man who—as my friend Calvin Thomsen says—has been raised on industrial-strength Adventism? He says to you, "If you really want to be saved, you will have to achieve a state of last-generation sinless perfection."

"But what about Jesus?" you ask. "Where does He fit in?"

"Well," they say, "yes. Yes. He fits in. But, to be honest, I'm not sure just how. He's kind of indistinct, fuzzy, hazy."

You say, "Where the Spirit of Jesus has really done His work, the role of Jesus can be seen with stunning clarity."

Have you met a Seventh-day Adventist in need of the second touch of Jesus?

You stand beside the widow at the gravesite. Others have drifted away. She's lingering, delaying the inevitable good-bye. And then she looks at you—her pastor—through tear-dimmed eyes. "I just keep hoping, keep praying, that I can be ready. Otherwise I'll never see him again."

And you stand there, remembering the Spirit's second touch in your own heart. You put your arm around her shoulder and say, "Do you know what the Word of Jesus says? It says that the One—*the One*—who began a good work in you will carry it to completion by the day of Jesus Christ."

Then you say to her, "I read that many times. But it wasn't until I read it one day through the touch of the Spirit that I realized what it meant. It means that Jesus says, 'What I start, I will finish!' It means that the Spirit is offering you the freedom to rest *right now* in that confidence *because of Jesus*."

> It says that the One— *the One*—who began a good work in you will carry it to completion by the day of Jesus Christ.

Have you met a Seventh-day Adventist in need of the second touch of Jesus? You'll know it when you meet them. You'll know it because no matter what they say, what they are *really* saying is just one thing: "I *see* Jesus. It's just that He's indistinct, blurry, hazy, like a tree, walking. I'm just not sure where He fits in."

Back in my early days in children's Sabbath school, we were asked, "Why do you want to go to heaven?" You remember that question. "What do you want to do when you get there?" And you remember the answer. "I want to ride a lion." "I want to slide down the neck of a giraffe." "I want to ski on the sea of glass." Remember those answers?

For the One

My answer to that question is different today. Is it the theological books I've read? Is it the children we've raised? Is it the gray in my beard? Or is it—could it be—that somewhere, somehow, one day, along the road of life, the hand of Jesus touched me a second time? Now, it wasn't just morality that was important. Now, what was important was *Him*.

So if you ask me that question today, "Why do you want to go to heaven?" I will tell you my answer in the words of the B J Thomas song:

> I've never seen the Eiffel Tower.
> I've never seen the streets of Rome.
> I've never seen the world's seven wonders,
> But I'll see the greatest wonder that day when I go home.
>
> 'Cause I'm gonna see Jesus, I'm gonna see Jesus.
> I'll see Him smile, open His arms and walk my way
> I'm gonna see Jesus, I'm gonna see Jesus
> I'm gonna look into His eyes someday.[2]

---

1. Brad & Dee McIntyre, "The Adventist Blues," recorded in 1978.

2. B J Thomas, "I'm Gonna See Jesus," written by Jordan/Archie Paul, © Universal Music Publishing Group, 2009.

Phylacteries

Celebrate, remember, love

David Franklin

It was the last line of defense, the final barrier between the rushing volcanic fury of oil and gas and one of the worst environmental disasters in United States history.

Its very name—the blind shear ram—suggested its blunt purpose. When all else failed, if the crew of the Deepwater Horizon oil rig lost control of a well, if a dreaded blowout came, the blind shear ram's two tough blades were poised to slice through the drill pipe, seal the well and save the day. Everything else could go wrong, just so long as "the pinchers" went right. All it took was one mighty stroke.

On the night of April 20, 2010, minutes after an enormous blowout ripped through the Deepwater Horizon, the rig's desperate crew pinned all hope on this last line of defense.

But the line did not hold.

An examination by the *New York Times* highlights the chasm between the oil industry's assertions about the reliability of its blowout preventers and a more complex reality. It reveals that the federal agency charged with regulating offshore drilling—the Minerals Management Service—repeatedly declined to act on advice from its own experts on how it could minimize the risk of a blind shear ram failure.

David J Hayes, the deputy interior secretary, said, "What happened to all the stakeholders—Congress, environmental groups, industry, the government—all stakeholders involved were lulled into a sense of what has turned out to be false security."[1]

For the One

This explains how one of the worst environmental disasters in United States history occurred. The Deepwater Horizon oil spill gushed into the Gulf of Mexico for 87 days, spilling an estimated 5 million barrels of oil into the sea and killing 11 workers.[2] It appears the oil spill was caused by failure of a failsafe—the blind shear ram. Once activated, the blind shear ram was to cut the oil pipe and prevent the oil from spilling into the ocean. But this failsafe system failed.

However, the article reveals a more "complex" reality than a simple mechanical malfunction. The failsafe did fail but the question is why. The article shares with us that officials failed to check the system and evaluate its ability to perform the task for which it was created. Advice was given, but the evaluators failed to heed the advice having a "false security" that their failsafe system was secure. They took pride in having the system, rather than evaluating its effectiveness. And when they needed it most, the failsafe failed.

Generally speaking, machines that can destroy life and/or damage the environment are created with a failsafe or failsafe system. So that, in the event of a failure, the machine will shut off, reset to default mode, turn on autopilot or even self-destruct in order to preserve life and prevent—to the best of its ability—irreplaceable loss.

So wouldn't it be good if there were a spiritual failsafe? Wouldn't it be cool if our spiritual lives were failsafe? If, in the event of a spiritual failure or a failure of our religious system, we could rely on some device, some procedure, some process, some protocol, some angel, some teaching, some reality to save us from spiritual corruption and depravity?

Reminder

In Exodus 13, it seems God provided such a system. After delivering the children of Israel from Egyptian bondage in the most miraculous way, God instituted the Feast of Unleavened Bread and the Passover, saying, "This observance will be for you like a sign on your hand and a reminder on your forehead that this law of the Lord is to be on your lips. For the Lord brought you out of Egypt with his mighty hand" (verse 9, NIV).

Notice the word: reminder.

Jesus in Our Theology

Verse 16 of the same chapter repeats a similar idea about this celebration saying, "And it will be like a sign on your hand and a symbol on your forehead that the Lord brought us out of Egypt with his mighty hand."

Notice the word: symbol.

Two passages in Deuteronomy add to the substance of what this symbol was intended to remind the children of Israel to do. Namely, in Deuteronomy 6, to "Love the Lord your God with all your heart, soul, and strength." And again the admonition is given: "Tie them as symbols on your hands and bind them on your foreheads."

Deuteronomy 11 adds the promise of blessings if the children of Israel are careful to obey the command "to love the Lord your God and serve him with all your heart and with all your soul" (verse 13, NIV), God promises to send rain on the land and provide grass for the cattle and crops to their satisfaction. And in verse 18—for the fourth and final time in the Pentateuch—the children of Israel are encouraged to "fix these words of mine in your hearts and minds; tie them as symbols on your hands and bind them on your foreheads."

So we have the commands to: celebrate, remember and love.

> Regularly rehearsing God's mighty deliverance from Egyptian bondage would inspire the children of Israel to love God.

It is clear one helps the other. Regularly rehearsing God's mighty deliverance from Egyptian bondage would inspire the children of Israel to love God. And their love for God would help them to regularly rehearse past blessings and the promise of future ones.

In this way, these four passages of scripture—Exodus 13:1–10, Exodus 13:11–16, Deuteronomy 6:4–9 and Deuteronomy 11:13–21—constituted a spiritual failsafe system for the children of Israel. The system was intended to preserve the children of Israel should a spiritual blowout occur. In the event they lost their way or they were drawn away to worship other gods or in consorting with heathen nations they picked up ungodly practices, the yearly celebration and remembrance

For the One

of God delivering them from Egypt and the daily commitment to love God with their heart, mind and soul should have prevented them from totally losing their way. It should have prevented spiritual failure.

But the failsafe system failed.

Failure

By the time Jesus enters the story, instead of the failsafe system reminding God's people of His mighty outstretched arm and turning their hearts to back Him, it had become a sign of spiritual pedigree. The children of Israel developed a false sense of security in their system of rules, regulations, rituals, and rites. They placed their faith in having the system, rather than the God who created the system. The leaders were using the forms of the system to show their piety rather than renew the reality of a life surrendered to God. That which was supposed to be a renewable resource continuously recalibrating their hearts back to God, simply became an outward declaration of who's better than who.

This reality is prominently illustrated by the literal application of the common refrain in the scriptures noted earlier. The command to tie "as symbols" on your hands and bind them on your foreheads was taken literally.

Enter phylacteries—also known as *Tefillin*—small black prayer boxes affixed to the weak arm and forehead. Each box contained four passages of scripture: Exodus 13:1–10, Exodus 13:11–16, Deuteronomy 6:4–9, Deuteronomy 11:13–21.

Then and now, Jews utilized the phylacteries in their Morning Prayer. First a prayerful meditation is rehearsed, then a special blessing is pronounced as each phylactery is put on, one for the arm and another for the forehead.

The Standard Jewish Book of Prayer's meditation before laying on the Phylacteries gives some insight into the significance of this moment for Jews. Here's an excerpt:

> I am here intent upon the act of laying the Tefillin, in fulfillment of the command of my Creator, who hath commanded us to lay the Tefillin, as it is written in the Law. . . . Within these Tefillin are placed four sections of the Law,

Jesus in Our Theology

> that declare the absolute unity of God, and that remind us of the miracles and wonders which he wrought for us when he brought us forth from Egypt, even he who hath power over the highest and the lowest to deal with them according to his will. . . . May the effect of the precept thus observed be to extend to me long life with sacred influences and holy thoughts, free from every approach, even in imagination, to sin and iniquity. . . . Amen.

So far so good. The remembrance of God's work surely could not be a bad idea. And if putting on a box helps to you do that, so be it.

In fact, a meditative prayer like this might be useful for us also. We might pray,

> Lord, we thank you for bringing us through the dark moments of 1844. You led us beyond the struggle and the disappointment that shook us to our very core. May this sublime reality keep us from dividing into separate camps and alienating ourselves from the world. May we extend to everyone we encounter the grace You have bestowed on us. Keep us from every evil inclination, but may we be led to serve you as Lord with all of our heart, mind, and soul.

> **He points to the intent of some to display their spirituality by what's on their head, rather than what's in their heart.**

Surely a prayer such as this could assist us in drawing closer to God. Anything that takes our attention off the form and points us to the Formula Maker is a good thing. And it is well within the concept behind the admonition given in our failsafe passages to the children of Israel to tie the commands of God on their hand and bind them on their forehead. God wanted these commands to be lodged in their heart and mind and if certain practices helped them achieve that, good.

Jesus does not take issue with the phylacteries themselves. Rather, He points to the intent of some to display their spirituality by what's on their head, rather than what's in their heart. Specifically, Jesus points to their unnecessary practice of broadening their phylacteries for everyone

For the One

to see. Clearly, the purpose was no longer to provide a constant reminder to themselves of the goodness and grace of God but rather to "prove" to everyone else how holy they were.

Our "phylacteries"

I wonder if we, as a church community, are not plagued by a similar condition. Not necessarily for prominence but possibly for approval. While I would certainly not purport that spiritual elitism is absent from our denomination, I wonder if it might be parading around as spiritual minimalism. I wonder if the fear of being viewed as unorthodox—not Adventist enough—has pushed to us wear our spirituality in our meatless dinner plates, our drumless worship, and our womenless pulpits.

I also wonder if the fear of being viewed as too orthodox—or too Adventist, "old school' or "traditional"—has pushed to wear our spirituality in our Sabbath-school quarterly-less Sabbath School classes, Revelation-less preaching, and hymn-less singing.

Here's my question: Are we so bent on proving how right and holy we are, that we have voided our lives and our communities of the very practices that create an authentic relationship with God? Are we emphasizing our practices, standards, teachings, and doctrines, as a tool to prove spirituality, or as a way to rediscover over and over again the grace of God?

In as much as our choice to take hymns out of our worship or only sing them exclusively, in as much as our choice to stray away from preaching Revelation or solely preach from Revelation every opportunity we get, in as much as our choice to attend The One Project or to avoid this Jesus-loving gathering, in as much as our choices have the intent of proving ourselves more righteous than other people, we are wearing our spirituality on our head and not in our heart.

In other words, we are broadening our phylacteries.

We do this because we want to be able to say we are not like *them*—whomever "them" is. But remember the parable Jesus told about the Pharisee and the Tax Collector in Luke 18. The man who went home justified was not the man who thanked God because he could prove his religious orthodoxy *by* what he had done, but rather the man who cried out for mercy *because* of what he had done. The tax collector's humility connected him to God. The Pharisee's proof left him unjustified before God.

We must not let our doctrines and teachings be reduced to tools used to create a wedge between others and us. Our doctrines must be a link that continues to give us a clearer picture of Jesus and invites others to come and see what we have discovered.

But the desire to prove ourselves goes way back in our denomination's history. In the aftermath of 1844, the group of Millerite Advent believers in the midst of their disappointment were scrambling to figure out what went wrong and to prove to the Christian community and the world that our beliefs were based on the word of God. Our early publications were filled with "Our Present Position," "The Sabbath Instituted at Creation" and proof that the 1844 dating was not incorrect.[3] We wanted to prove we were not a cult, we were people of God, and we were specially called to this troubling experience in order to share the full truth with the world.

It is interesting that William Barclay notes that the sect of Judaism known as the Pharisees started for a similar reason. He describes how the Pharisees arose in response to the introduction of Greek culture and religion into society: "Faced with the threat directed against [the Jewish faith], they determined to spend their whole lives in one long observance of Judaism in its most elaborate and ceremonial and legal form."[4]

> The desire to prove ourselves goes way back in our denomination's history.

Is it possible the energy expended to prove our orthodoxy to the community at large has overflowed into proving our orthodoxy to the various factions within our very own denomination?

Is it possible our fears of being labeled something we are not has pushed us to one extreme or another? Is it possible we have worn our beliefs like badges of honor, intent on proving whatever camp we stand in as right, while sacrificing the transformational value that these beliefs can produce in our lives?

For the One

If we are going to boast

Our doctrinal and cultural uniqueness was not given to us to prove our spiritual orthodoxy to anyone. It was given to us that we might remember the grace of God in our lives and share that gift of grace with everyone we encounter.

We must not let our history divide us into Adventist political parties, where we preach sermons and support initiatives that play to our base. Rather, our history must be the legacy that reminds us of the amazing miracles that God's outstretched arm has done in our community. We must view our history as the portal through which we see a personal Jesus who cared about this small group of Advent believers and nurtured us from a fledgling scattered group to a worldwide movement.

We must not become arrogant with the truth entrusted to us. Let's not let the little we do know become a platform for boasting.

Let's boast because we know Jesus. Let's boast because the truth we do have has led us to have radical encounters with Him and has transformed our lives.

If we are going to boast, let's boast because the Jesus we know helps us wrestle with tough issues in a way in which we are all actually listening to one another and having God-honoring, transformational dialogue—even if we never totally agree.

If we are going to boast, let's boast because we are living in communities and worshipping at churches where we are overcoming bias, bigotry, hatred, division, and deceit.

If we are going to boast, let's boast because remembering and keeping the Sabbath makes us more loving, kind and peaceful.

If we are going to boast, let's boast because we are experiencing the outpouring of the Holy Spirit.

If we are going to boast, let's boast because we are walking so close with God that every now and then we can almost see the chariots that came to take Elijah.

If we are going to boast, let's boast because we have overcome the tendency to divide ourselves and separate ourselves and isolate ourselves and preach to ourselves and evangelize ourselves.

If we are going to boast, let's boast that 70 per cent of young adults

Jesus in Our Theology

who grew up in the church are staying in the church, rather than leaving like they do today.

If we are going to boast, let's boast that the divorce rate in the church doesn't match the divorce rate outside of the church.

If we are going to boast, let's boast that in every city where there is a Seventh-day Adventist church there is a statistically lower crime rate, poverty rate and secondary school drop-out rate.

If we are going to boast, let's boast only over those things that will bring glory to the name and the cause of God.

Until then, let's humble ourselves and praise God that He hasn't given up on us yet. And rehearse His goodness to us as a church and as individuals.

Our failsafe

God has given to us a spiritual failsafe to keep us from becoming enamored with our phylacteries and dividing ourselves based on spiritual pedigree. It's a failsafe system that will fight off the tendency to acquiesce because of the fear of being labeled and isolated.

It's pretty simple:

> Celebrate.
>
> Remember.
>
> Love.

> If we are going to boast, let's boast only over those things that will bring glory to the name and the cause of God.

I think we are doing pretty good with the "Remember" part but we could use some improvement with the "Celebrating" and "Loving."

When we use our doctrinal and cultural distinctives to remind us of the work of Jesus in our lives, celebrate His continuing deliverance, and drive us to deepen our love for Him and for others, we move our religion from our head to our heart.

Let's make sure our failsafe holds.

For the One

1. *New York Times*, June 20, 2010, authors David Barstow, Laura Dodd, James Glanz, Stephanie Saul, and Ian Urbina.

2. <www.time.com/time/specials/packages/article/0,28804,2035319_2035315_2035680,00.html>.

3. "Learned opponents did not, and could not, show that we were incorrect in dating the 2300 days from BC 457. With this clearly ascertained date for the commencement of the main pillar of the 'original' Advent faith, lecturers went forth united to give the judgment hour cry" (*Second Advent Review & Sabbath Herald*, December 1850).

The Heresy Response

Jesus our Content

Tim Gillespie

We Adventists are good at teaching certain things. Perhaps the thing we are best at teaching is the context of our faith communities, traditions, and our lifestyles. We have become experts at who we are, how we live, and how we transfer that knowledge to the next generation. And these are all good things.

But sometimes, because of the *context*, we never get to the *Content*. And it seems like even when we experience the context everyday, we still preach that. For example, have you ever been in church and heard a sermon on why the Sabbath is right . . . in church, on Sabbath? That seems a bit redundant.

Until our preaching transcends our context and gets to our content, which—I probably don't have to remind you—is Jesus, we are teetering dangerously close to a narcissistic idolatry that can be called heresy.

But let me give you some context for this argument.

The Christological heresy

We belong to the great tradition and greater trajectory of orthodox Christian thought. And in 2000 years, there has been but one Christological heresy expressed in two ways:

1. That which diminishes Jesus, His place, His divinity, His power or His sacrifice on the cross; and

For the One

2. That which leads to the withered fruit of less love.

We seem to have this pronounced response to Jesus. First comes acceptance and joy, the peace of being saved through the cross of Christ.

Although we are not saved by the cross, but through the work of Jesus on it. A cross without a Christ is nothing more than a badly built piece of furniture. But with Jesus it becomes the plan of salvation, a symbol that was literally wrenched from the Romans and given to the kingdom of God.

But soon comes the buyer's remorse, the pushback. It's the difference between "Jesus paid it all" and "Can I get that on layaway?"

The question becomes "Where do I fit in?"—and we ask it corporately by saying "Where do we fit in? As Adventists, what is our role?" We are either uncomfortable with the totality of the cross of Christ, or we are uncomfortable with our place in the shadow of it. We somehow want to bring Jesus off the cross

And, eventually, we try and find our way onto it.

Because the cross of Jesus couldn't possibly be enough. It couldn't possibly give me enough identity, enough peace, enough grace, or enough salvation.

So we scream that age-old question: "What must I do to be saved?" But maybe what we really mean is "What must I do to be a *special*?" Then we create theology around this question.

"The Measuring Rod"

If you grew up around the Adventist church in a certain era, you might well remember a story called "The Measuring Rod." I can't remember it all, which might be due to my inability to remember anything that scared me in my childhood. However, as I remember it, the story is that a man had a dream about Jesus coming again, and how Jesus had a measuring rod that was set up in the middle of the town. After a while, the name of someone in the town would be called, and that person would come and stand next to the measuring rod. The rod would grow or shrink—or perhaps they would—according to the works that the individual had done in his or her life.

I can remember hearing that story and being frightened. I was frightened of a God who would judge each of us according to this "measuring rod."

But now I am a bit older and a bit wiser, and I have read the Gospels of Jesus Christ, and lingered long in the epistles of Paul, and have discovered the grace and joy that is the revelation of Jesus Christ found in that final book of the Bible. And I've come to know at least one thing: There is only one measuring rod, and it is the cross of Jesus Christ.

Perhaps Jürgen Moltmann said it best when he stated:

> And for me that meant, whatever can stand before the face of the crucified Christ is true Christian Theology. What cannot stand there must disappear. This is especially true of what we say about God. . . . In Christianity, the cross is the test of everything which deserves to be called Christian.[1]

All heresy begins when we choose a different measuring rod for anything, for everything. "Jesus. All." means all that Jesus did, and we have an apex of that work at the cross. We make a mistake when we think that in Christian theology there is a level playing field. Belying a "flatland" theology, it all moves toward or results from the cross of Jesus Christ.

> All heresy begins when we choose a different measuring rod for anything, for everything.

Taking offense

But perhaps this heretical response of ours makes sense. We always respond to the cross by trying to get Jesus off of the cross. At a DNA level we know He doesn't belong there. It has to be repugnant and offensive. That is the power of the cross.

That which is anathema is true—and then it saves you!

We try to tear Him down because we are uncomfortable with the picture. Or because we think there might be room for us up there. Or because we think He needs our help to save us.

But there is not room on the cross for two.

However, there is room in its shadow for everyone who ever has, does or ever will live.

For the One

At the same time, we don't like to owe anyone anything. So we come up with ways to settle the debt. We have a tendency to stack works upon works in an effort to build a ladder to heaven, when the way has already been built and bridged by the cross of Christ. The truth is that it is the indebtedness that sets us free.

This heretical response to Jesus, to His life and death, the cross and His resurrection can become so institutionalized within one's theology that it no longer feels like heresy. But then it becomes a question of trajectory—where this group of people are going, due to how they hold Jesus within their theology.

Beyond theology

But it is not theology that saves us. Jesus holds that place. Our theology continues to be the way we express our best thoughts about Jesus but Jesus is not bound by our words. He always transcends them. He lives beyond them, in a realm of meaning we can hardly comprehend. So we use these units of thought that we call words to explain, describe, and try to capture the mystery of Jesus. However, our words fail us—and they always will.

The danger is that we somehow become enamored by our words more than the cross and believe somehow it is our words that save us, even our words about Him. Even though our theology is a good thing, if held in the wrong way, it becomes a dangerous thing.

One of the purposes of the gospel of John was a response to the heresy that was, from a very early point, creeping into the thought process of the church. John takes this heresy on from the very first word:

> In the beginning was the Word, and the Word was with God, and the Word was God. He was with God in the beginning. Through him all things were made; without him nothing was made that has been made. In him was life, and that life was the light of all mankind (John 1:1–4, NIV).

He puts Jesus right where He needs to be—and keeps saying it in the following verses and throughout his book—rebutting our tendency to put ourselves in places we shouldn't be.

Jesus in Our Theology

The testimony of John

> After this, Jesus and his disciples went out into the Judean countryside, where he spent some time with them, and baptized. Now John also was baptizing at Aenon near Salim, because there was plenty of water, and people were coming and being baptized. (This was before John was put in prison.) An argument developed between some of John's disciples and a certain Jew over the matter of ceremonial washing. They came to John and said to him, "Rabbi, that man who was with you on the other side of the Jordan—the one you testified about—look, he is baptizing, and everyone is going to him" (John 3:22–26, NIV).

People had connected with John. They responded to his preaching. In today's terms, he was running an independent ministry that was booming. He was drawing the crowds and counting up the baptisms. They let him have his idiosyncrasies because he was so good at preparing the way.

But after Jesus had begun His ministry, some people were still following John. John had provided the context into which Jesus might come, but there were those who were still following the context, not moving on to the Content to Whom John had pointed.

> There were those who were still following the context, not moving on to the Content to Whom John had pointed.

So John's followers were arguing, it seems, with someone who had not accepted Jesus. Somehow, in the midst of the conversation about ceremonial washing, this Jesus guy came up, and it really irked the disciples of John. They were upset that people weren't following John. So they went to John and tried to get him to agree with them that what was happening on the other side of the river was going to somehow ruin everything he had built.

But John had an answer to this:

> To this John replied, "*A person can receive only what is given them from heaven.* You yourselves can testify that I said, 'I am not the Messiah but am sent ahead of him.' The bride

For the One

belongs to the bridegroom. The friend who attends the bridegroom waits and listens for him, and is full of joy when he hears the bridegroom's voice. That joy is mine, and it is now complete (John 3:27–29, NIV, emphasis added).

That first phrase puts things in perspective. We can't consume more than what we are given. And John knew what he had been given.

And then he reminded them what his content had always been. He never claimed a place on the cross, only that there was a cross and the One coming would occupy it. His message is consistent. He never steps out of his role, the proclamation of the One to come. Even when Jesus had come, John knew his place.

As Christians—and I ask this honestly—is there any other place to be than proclaiming Him as the most important thing the world has ever seen? Isn't this the call of those who believe in Jesus? Could there be a more dangerous place to be than where we are proclaiming something else to be more important than Jesus? Is any Christian, any Christian community, in danger of becoming like those disciples of John when they say that there is another message that supersedes Jesus? These are just a few of the questions I have.

The ultimate response

But John continues, with eight words that make all the difference in the world. He says the words that fix our theological and behavioral narcissism. He says the words that combat all of heresy, all idolatry, all the problems we have as Christians in our relationships, in our communities, and in our theology:

"He must become greater; I must become less" (John 3:30, NIV).

That's it. That's the response to heresy. When it rears it's ugly head through perfectionism, exclusivist remnant theology, last-generation theology, date-setting or just the general heresy of Christians not loving others, there is only one response.

Any theology that leads to more of us and less of Him is teetering on the brink of heresy. Even our reading of scripture needs to be the revelation of Jesus Christ, not simply a road map of how we are supposed to live. Our understanding of us comes from a better understanding of Him. If we can continue to increase Jesus in our lives, our lives conform to Him.

He must become greater.
In our worship, He must become greater.
In our communities, He must become greater.
In our study, He must become greater.
In our marriages and families, He must become greater.
In our careers, He must become greater.
In our traditions, He must become greater.
in our trajectories, He must become greater.
In our faithfulness, He must become greater.
In our context, He must become greater.
And, in our content, He must become greater.

> Our understanding of us comes from a better understanding of Him.

1. Jürgen Moltmann (1974), *The Crucified God: The Cross of Christ as the Foundation and Criticism of Christian Theology*, Fortress Press, 1993, pages x, 7.

Jesus in Our Practice

Jesus
Rabbi. Healer.
Chronicler. Rebel.

Dilys Brooks

In 2000, Robert McIver penned *The Four Faces of Jesus: Four Gospel Writers, Four Unique Perspectives, Four Personal Encounters, One Complete Picture*, describing how the four gospels reflect different aspects of Jesus' ministry.[1] Over the past six years, I have read the Gospels—Matthew, Mark, Luke and John—as a part of my daily reflection and I can concur with McIver that each of the gospels does give a unique perspective about Jesus.

If I were to take a poll of people's perceptions or descriptors of Jesus, there would be some that we would agree on—Savior, healer, teacher, shepherd, friend—yet others might present different aspects of Jesus that we may or may not have experienced or agree with.

As I have spent the time working my way through the four gospels, Luke's story of Jesus is the one that draws me in time and time again. But it was to my chagrin that the passage I want to reflect on here was not a story on my radar. Somehow in my reading and re-reading of Luke, I simply missed it.

But in the story of Jesus healing a crippled woman recorded in Luke 13:10–17, Jesus seems to be doing what He always does and I am drawn to "four faces"—to borrow the term—or four words that describe Jesus: Rabbi. Healer. Chronicler. Rebel.

Can four words adequately describe He who is the I Am? I readily admit they do not, yet I propose these four words not only to tickle your mind, but also to challenge my own reflections on or about Jesus.

For the One

Reading Luke's account of Jesus, which is filled with the mounting tension between Jesus and the religious elite, helps me better understand the animosity and anger that met Him in Pilate's court that fateful day. When His people, the ones He had come to save cried out, "Give us Barabbas!" and He said nothing.

I submit these four words not to diminish what He came to do, but to challenge our reflection on who we ought to be as His followers. It is important to look at Jesus through the lens of *History*. Lisa Clark Diller—our resident historian—would say we need to know the context, circumstances, community, the sights, and sounds to ensure our decision to follow Jesus is not just an emotional or illogical one. We must be clear that in choosing to associate with this Jesus, we are also prepared to be like Jesus. Faith by association is not enough. Our faith must be the result of a committed growing, personal relationship with Jesus Christ.

Rabbi

The story in Luke 13:10–17 begins with Jesus in a familiar place doing a familiar thing: *He is teaching in the synagogue*. This had become Jesus' custom after His baptism by His cousin John, and the anointing by the Holy Spirit in the Jordan River after His sojourn in the wilderness where He defeated Satan (see Luke 4:14, 15).

It was His pattern of behavior to be in the synagogue teaching from the scriptures. The synagogue or meeting place played a significant role in Judaism. Unlike the temple, synagogues were located in all parts of the land. In the synagogue, there was no altar, and prayer and the reading of the Torah took the place of the sacrifice.[2]

Luke does not refer to Jesus as Rabbi, he uses the Greek word *epistates*,[3] the equivalent of "schoolmaster," a term more meaningful to his predominantly Greek readers (see Luke 17:13). Those who listened to Jesus took note of the authority with which He read and taught from the scriptures. Other rabbis or master teachers would refer to Moses as they expounded on the text but Jesus would often say, "I say to you . . ."

When we gather each week at our "synagogue," we submit to the teaching of the scripture from our "rabbis" but Jesus also invites each of us to become like Him, master teachers of the scriptures not just in the meeting place of the believers, but also in our homes and other places and spaces He provides for us. As Christ followers, it is not just the call of the pastor, elders or Sabbath school teachers to teach about Jesus. We all are commissioned to teach the word of God with authority and power (see Matthew 28:18–20).

Healer

We continue reading from Luke 13:

> And there was a woman who for eighteen years had had a sickness caused by a spirit; and she was bent double, and could not straighten up at all. When Jesus saw her, He called her over and said to her, "Woman, you are freed from your sickness." And He laid His hands on her; and immediately she was made erect again and began glorifying God (verses 11–13, NASB).

This woman was unique among all the women gathered for worship that Sabbath morning. She was bent double, unable to straighten up, and this condition had been her lot for the past 18 years. It doesn't appear that this woman is a stranger to this gathering because there is no reaction to her arrival or presence in the gathering. It seems they don't really "see" her in their midst.

> Once He takes notice of her, He segued from His role as a Rabbi to Healer.

But Jesus' reaction to her arrival catches my attention. He *saw* her. Once He took notice of her, He segued from His role as a Rabbi to Healer. There is no announcement of this change; it was a seamless transition as He inquiried about her condition. This interaction and several others reflect the role Isaiah prophetically described the Messiah as One who would "preach good news to the poor, . . . proclaim freedom for the prisoners and recovery of sight for the blind, [and] release the oppressed" (Luke 4:18, see also Isaiah 61:1, 2).

Jesus noticed the woman, called her over and proceeded to fulfill this scripture before the onlookers. I am convinced that Jesus would not teach about God when there were people who were sick or enslaved

For the One

to the bondages of sin in His presence. He would attend to the healing first.

The woman shuffled over to Jesus and He said, "Woman you are free from your ailment." He then placed His hands on her and immediately she stood up straight as she was healed.

Why did Jesus touch her after declaring her deliverance? Modern scientists would tell us that the skin is our body's largest organ, and when its sensory receptors are stimulated, the hormone oxytocin—the one that makes us feel good—is released. At the same time, cortisol—the stress hormone—is reduced.

So I think Jesus touched this woman to make her feel good! No-one knows how long it had been since someone had touched her or made her feel loved and valued.

So where are the healers in our churches? Where are the people who see the sick and bound ones in our midst and speak a word or offer a healing touch? Have you met them in your synagogue?

If we haven't seen these "healers" at work among us, perhaps it is because we suffer from eye disease. We are blinded from the maladies of our brothers and sisters in Christ because those who are ill wear a mask or we are so self-absorbed and self-centered that we have eyes only for ourselves.

Spiritual blindness can creep up on us unawares when our central vision—Jesus—is lost and we gradually lose sight of each other. If we would simply ask for new vision, we could see. If we simply ask Him for the power, He would then make us the healers we have been called to be.

Thankfully, there are people with the gift of healing who can be found among us. They are the people who greet us with Sabbath hugs, or pray with us when we ask for prayer. They are the people who listen to our fears, challenges, worries, and doubts. They are the people who discern when we are wearing a mask or putting on a good show, hoping no-one will see us as we really are. Our churches should be full of such healers!

Jesus is calling each of us to become those healers in our faith communities. He wants us to be uneasy when we encounter people crippled with anger, fear, abuse, envy or pride. Jesus wants us to interrupt our worship, study or our spiritual demonstrations when we

Jesus in Our Practice

are surrounded by those who have been under the bondage of Satan's attacks. Jesus may even give some of us the gift of healing, where we get to participate with Him in the miraculous deliverance of men, women, boys and girls from physical and spiritual sickness.

As a result of Jesus' healing touch, there was yet another adjustment to the order of service. What was the response of the woman who has been healed? She immediately stood up and began praising God! Exposition of scripture gave way to miraculous healing and now we see praise and worship the likes of which had never been experienced in this synagogue before.

Note the synagogue ruler's response: "But the synagogue official, indignant because Jesus had healed on the Sabbath, began saying to the crowd in response, 'There are six days in which work should be done; so come during them and get healed, and not on the Sabbath day'" (Luke 13:14).

His indignant response leads me to believe that nothing this miraculous has ever happened in this synagogue before. Which then begs the question, "Why isn't this a weekly occurrence?" Why aren't miracles happening during the times we gather each Sabbath to read scripture and pray together? It can't be because there aren't any people among us who are sick or doubled over under the attack of Satan.

> All they were supposed to do was read and reflect on the scripture, pray, and go home.

The answer to our questions is reflected in the synagogue ruler's retort. Healing was work and should be done on days one through six. He had literally pulled the plug on the worshipping and rejoicing directed toward God as a result of God's actions. He had shamed the people for their exuberance and rebuked the One who had performed the miracle. All they were supposed to do was read and reflect on the scripture, pray, and go home.

The sad thing about this ruler's reaction is that many of us would agree with him—if not in wording, in principle. We like to know what time our worship services will begin and end. We don't like to spend

For the One

too much time in "praise and worship," listening to testimonies or prayer requests. We have grown accustomed to an order of service and woe to anyone who tries to change it for the sake of doing something new or because they feel impressed by the Holy Spirit to do something differently.

Do you see the irony here? The leader rebuked He who made the planet, humanity and set aside the Sabbath as a day for rest. He reprimanded He who called Moses to the mountain and wrote the commandments with His own finger. He chastised the I AM!

The synagogue ruler was mindful of maintaining piety and order. He was zealous to maintain the sanctity of the place and time. We understand his reaction; he too suffered from spiritual blindness, which stopped him from seeing that he and Jesus were actually on the same side and desired the same end. Jesus also wanted to maintain the sanctity of the place and time.

While the synagogue was the place that the Jews in the diaspora gathered weekly because the temple had been destroyed, Sabbath becomes a *time* when we who have Christ in us gather to worship Him together. If there is any among us who is sick or troubled, we shouldn't wait until Sabbath is over to seek healing and deliverance. How much sweeter will our worship, adoration, and understanding of God be when we see Him actively engaged in the lives of believers? When we place limits on how God works on Sabbaths, we are in bondage to Satan and deny the power of God.

Chronicler

There was yet another change in the order of service. Jesus became the chronicler of the story of the children of Israel. We continue reading Luke 13:

> But the Lord answered him and said, "You hypocrites! Does not each of you on the Sabbath untie his ox or his donkey from the manger, and lead it away to give it water? And ought not this woman, a daughter of Abraham whom Satan bound for eighteen long years, be set free from this bondage on the Sabbath day?" (verses 15, 16).

It's as if Jesus said, "If we are going to be historical, let's be consistent."

Jesus in Our Practice

It is written, "You shall not see your countryman's donkey or his ox fallen down on the way, and pay no attention to them; you shall certainly help him to raise them up" (Deuteronomy 22:4, NASB, see also Exodus 23:4, 5).

On Sabbaths, oxen and donkeys were to be untied and led to water, how much more should a suffering daughter of Abraham be set free? Jesus took the entire congregation back to the origin of the Hebrew people. This woman wasn't simply a woman bound by Satan; she was a daughter of Abraham and her healing and deliverance on Sabbath was a revelation to all—including Satan—that Jesus is truly Lord of the Sabbath!

We can't forget the way sick people were treated or looked upon in the Ancient Near East. When someone suffered some type of physical malady, demon possession, leprosy or barrenness, it was believed to be a consequence of their sins or the sins of their parents. It was as if they deserved their maladies. When we no longer "see" people the way Jesus "sees" them—as the individuals He came to save from sin and death—we will also remain oblivious to their need of the Rabbi, Healer, Savior and Restorer—Jesus Christ.

> Wherever we are at, Jesus challenges us to write a *new* history of our lives.

In a sense, we are all chroniclers. Often we chronicle the wrongs we have committed against others or God and we have a good history of the hurts people have done to us. Some of us can trace our family connections within the context of Adventism back several generations, while some of us are new to this whole "Sevvie" way of life or even to Christianity.

Wherever we are at, Jesus challenges us to write a *new* history of our lives—one that begins on the day we accept what He did on Calvary to deliver us from the bondage of sin. We don't have to compare how sinful we are to each other, instead we should reflect on what God has done for all and each of us. Then with His help, we can write a new story, intertwined with the story of the children of Israel because we, too, are sons and daughters of Abraham.

Once we are clear about our story, we will better comprehend God's love for this planet, and it gives Him freedom to move through us in sharing this plan with the world. It also empowers us to write new stories that reflect a Savior alive and working in our world today.

When Jesus refered to this woman as a daughter of Abraham it brought the entire gathering back to the realization that she was in bondage but has now been truly set free. What was the response of the synagogue leader and others to Jesus' reproof? The story concludes: "When he said this, all his opponents were put to shame; and the entire crowd was rejoicing at all the wonderful things that he was doing" (Luke 13:17, NRSV).

Silence. Joy. Muteness from the detractors and true worship ensues.

Rebel

There is one more name or face of Jesus that becomes evident in this story sequence found in Luke 13. Jesus also rebelled against the Jewish expectation of who the Messiah should be. The descendants of Israel were looking and preparing for a Savior who would be a Warrior-King. One Bible commentator states,

> Yet everything about Jesus' ministry controverted their understanding of who the Leader would be. Instead, Jesus tried to instill in their minds the prospect that the road to His future glory was bound to run by way of the cross, with its experience of rejection, suffering and humiliation.[4]

The gospels—especially Luke—are filled with this tension: Jesus' outright rebellion against the expectation of the religious right, Pharisees, Sadducees, priests, and even the common people, who were looking for a champion. Time and time again, Jesus disappointed them by His association with sinners and His willingness to break the rules regarding Sabbath.

Yet the descendants of Abraham were not the main target of Jesus' rebellion. His insurgency was primarily against the kingdom of Satan. This story reflects His unwillingness to allow Satan to hold any son or daughter of Abraham hostage. In freeing this woman, He foreshadowed how He would ultimately free all humanity from sickness, death, hell, and the grave, once and for all.

It's not simply that we are saved and need to stay saved. Rather, we are a part of an army of believers who are declaring that business-as-usual is unacceptable for this planet. Jesus calls us to be rebels. Rebels against Satan, sin, and the status quo. Against an understanding of who God is that is not vibrant, growing or progressive.

We must not fall into the trap of believing that we have a complete knowledge of the revelation of God. We must leave room for the Holy Spirit to do new things and give us new experiences. We must also be open to have Him work through us to do new things.

Four callings

Thus we have seen four faces of Jesus: Rabbi, Healer, Chronicler, and Rebel.

Will you become a teacher? I hope you will.

We can't be satisfied with listening to messages, week after week, which keep us preoccupied with interpreting the signs of the times or cause us to be like the synagogue leader, so preoccupied with defending God's laws at the cost of the deliverance and healing of the walking wounded God leads into our midst. We must become the teachers, whose lives reflect a submitted and dependent life centered in Jesus.

> We must leave room for the Holy Spirit to do new things and give us new experiences.

Will you become a healer? I hope you will.

Healing is not reserved for those who are most spiritual among us. James 5:17 urges us to call for the elders and become intercessors. There is no reason for us to wonder if we can pray for healing or deliverance for those who are under Satan's attacks. We are called to be the healers of emotional, physical, and spiritual sickness, both in the body of Christ and certainly outside of the body.

Will you begin to chronicle a new story? I hope you will.

It isn't enough for us to be chroniclers of the Judeo-Christian faith where we can repeat with accuracy the history, purpose, and doctrines of our denomination. It isn't enough for us to be able to articulate our own Christian experience through the lens of Adventism with prophetic

For the One

clarity. We don't get "stars" because we knew the doctrines and kept them all. We must be more than reflectors of other men or women's thoughts, no matter how truthful they may be.

Will you join in the rebellion? I hope you will.

We must rebel against doing church the way we have always done it. We must not fall into the trap of Abraham's sons and daughters where we believe that God isn't moving because of something we haven't done. Jesus' first advent revealed that He came in the fullness of time and He will return in the fullness of time. What we do with our time is what we will be judged on. Will we set up more rules and regulations to preserve the integrity of the remnant? Or will we ask Yeshua—the Messiah of the remnant—what He wants us to do, then obey? We must join the rebellion against Satan and his kingdom because he has already been defeated and there are other sons and daughters of Abraham out in the world who need to experience Jesus' healing and deliverance from sin.

Maybe if we become Rabbis, Healers, Chroniclers, and Rebels, our Sabbath gatherings would become a time and place for healing, deliverance, praise, and worship, not just the place we show up because we got the day right.

1. Robert McIver, *The Four Faces of Jesus*, Pacific Press Publishing Association, 2000.

2. C L Feinberg, "Synagogue" in D R W Wood, I H Marshall, A R Millard, J I Packer & D J Wiseman (editors), *New Bible Dictionary* (third edition), InterVarsity Press, 1996.

3. R Stagg, "Rabbi" in C Brand, C Draper, A England, S Bond, E R Clendenen & T C Butler (editors), *Holman Illustrated Bible Dictionary*, Holman Bible Publishers. 2003.

4. R P Martin, "Messiah" in *Holman Illustrated Bible Dictionary*, op cit.

Hens and Chicks

The leadership of Jesus

Timothy Nixon

One of the doctrines of Jesus we have failed to recognize or develop in the church is Jesus' teaching on leadership. Jesus taught His disciples an ethic, a doctrine of leadership that appeared throughout His life and ministry. He was very specific in drawing the contrast between the world's understanding of leadership and His kingdom's understanding of leadership.

From His own example of condescension to His private and public discourses, Jesus taught a consistent principle of leadership. It was an ethic that directly challenged the hierarchical system of leadership and nepotism that existed in His day. And that example of leadership, which Jesus critiqued, was completely embraced and practiced by the religious leaders of Jerusalem. And because they had such great influence among the people as mediators between them and God, their leadership was regarded as normal by the masses of people. The notion that the higher you ascend, the less accessible you are to people—especially common people—was the ethic people embraced.

When James and John attempted to position themselves on Jesus' right and left, Jesus told them they did not know what they were asking for. If they wanted to pursue leadership in Jesus' kingdom, they first had to drink Christ's cup, then God would decide where they would sit. And I wonder how many who either aspire to or sit in leadership today are willing to drink the cup that Jesus drank.

And after that—leave it up to God to decide where you serve. In Christ's ethic of leadership, God determines what positions His followers hold in His kingdom.

His kingdom would not be hierarchical like the structures that distinguished the world's system of leadership. In Matthew 12:48—when His family came expecting a special place and position with Him—because they were His family, Jesus' response was, "Who is My family? Who are my brothers and sisters? Those who do My Father's will, these are my family." For Jesus, no position was based on progeny, privilege, position or gender.

The ethic of leadership that Jesus taught and practiced before His disciples—which He established as the principle of leadership for His kingdom and His followers—is servant leadership.

We all know it. It's much too clearly articulated and practiced by Jesus in the gospels for us not to know it. Yet nobody practices it. Nobody.

And I've heard people say things like, "That sounds good, but it's not practical."

"Jesus Only," "Jesus. All."—is it just slogan? Or does it go beyond a feel-good expression to a real-good experience?

Jesus' religion critique

It is significant that the final message Jesus presented to His disciples and the "church" in the temple courts of Jerusalem was His analysis of the church's leadership. And what an opportunity for the church to have. I am sure we would be fascinated to have Jesus' assessment of the leadership of the church and how it measures up to His principles.

So Jesus took on the Sanhedrin and gave the Jewish priesthood an analysis of their leadership. He was not concerned with the leadership of some off-shoot or radical outlandish movement, rather He zeroed in on the leadership of the church. In Matthew 23:1–12, He used explicit language to describe what He saw.

They had assumed the seat of Moses—Israel's greatest prophet. But they wanted the position God gave to Moses without the relationship God had with Moses. As Jesus looked at their leadership, He noticed a fundamental flaw. In effect, He said, "Do what they say—but not what they do." They were great interpreters of the law. Their orthodoxy and exegesis was impeccable but their practice was invisible. They laid heavy burdens on others that they did not carry themselves. And they did nothing to relieve others.

They gave justice with no mercy, condemnation without compassion.

Jesus in Our Practice

We are still big on condemning people without extending the grace to them that we need ourselves. We are reckless in our correction of people. Ellen White speaks of how we should correct others:

> I have seen the great sacrifice which Jesus made to redeem man. He did not consider His own life too dear to sacrifice. Said Jesus, "Love one another, as I have loved you." Do you feel, when a brother errs, that you could give your life to save him? If you feel thus, you can approach him and affect his heart; you are just the one to visit that brother. But it is a lamentable fact that many who profess to be brethren, are not willing to sacrifice any of their opinions or their judgments to save a brother. There is but little love for one another. A selfish spirit is manifested.[1]

Jesus also noticed how the leaders loved the place of honor. They liked to sit in the "chief" seats and to be addressed as "Rabbi." But again He brought His kingdom's contrast:

> But you are not to be called rabbi, for you have one teacher, and you are all brothers. And call no man your father on earth, for you have one Father, who is in heaven. Neither be called instructors, for you have one instructor, the Christ. The greatest among you shall be your servant. Whoever exalts himself will be humbled, and whoever humbles himself will be exalted (Matthew 23:8–12).

> **Greatness is not determined by self-promotion. Kingdom leadership is achieved through self-denial.**

Greatness is not determined by self-promotion. Kingdom leadership is achieved through self-denial and self-renunciation. Those who exalt themselves will be humbled—that's what Jesus said and that's the path to leadership in Christ's kingdom.

Yet we are constantly taught and trained to promote ourselves in order to get anywhere in life—including in the church. You have to put your name out there. You have to do something to be recognized. You have to know the right people and have an advocate to promote you and push your name.

For the One

So today whose method, whose ethic of leadership are we following?

And let's be specific: Whose method of leadership am I following? Are you following?

In my home, on my job, with my family, with my friends and neighbors, in the church—which one?

The heart of the problem

After this scathing critique of these religious leaders, Jesus spoke eight "woes," which make for fearful reading. But in one of those woes, Jesus gave the reason for the condition of the leadership in the "church" and He went to the heart of the problem:

> "Woe to you, scribes and Pharisees, hypocrites! For you clean the outside of the cup and the plate, but inside they are full of greed and self-indulgence. You blind Pharisee! First clean the inside of the cup and the plate, that the outside also may be clean" (Matthew 23:25, 26).

We can be so obsessed with externals, while leaving the inside unattended to. We might think the answer to a healthy spirituality is to pray more, to fast more, to study God's word, but it must be more than that. The Pharisee was doing that when he thanked God he was not like the publican (see Luke 18:9–14)—so it has to be more than that.

What reveals the emphasis in our lives is how we treat other people. It was not the priest and the Levite, who passed by the victim of misfortune, that Jesus used to exemplify His Kingdom. It was the Samaritan—who stopped and attended to his wounds, placed him on His donkey, found him a place to stay, and paid for his expenses (see Luke 10:30–37).

Jesus called them "the least of these." The ones who can't invite you to Sabbath dinner after you invite them. Who don't return your favors and can't return your phone calls. How we treat them reveals whether our Christianity is internal or merely external.

Jesus continued to explain how external-only results in religion that majors in minors (see Matthew 23:29–36). We can be tempted to make trivial matters important, focusing on things that do not merit our first affections. We can be careful about honoring dead prophets and

Jesus in Our Practice

cleaning their tombs, while plotting to crucify the One their prophecies pointed to.

Our problem is we think we know what's best for ourselves. We want to set the agenda and direction of the church. And what we want from Jesus is for Him to fall in line with us and to embrace our agenda. That was the mantra of the Scribes and Pharisees from the moment they encountered Christ's kingdom. First they tried to woo John the Baptist. And when Jesus came, they tried to bring Him under their direction.

What do you think Nicodemus was doing when He came to Jesus by night? They wanted to bring Jesus under their wings. The rabbis had a saying when a proselyte was won by them, describing it as "coming under the wings of the Shekinah." That's what they wanted from Jesus—for Him to fall in line with them.

But did Jesus come to follow them? I think sometimes we really believe that if Jesus came to this earth today that He would join *us*. But Jesus did not come to join them—He came so they could join Him.

He did not come to follow them. He came to lead them.

> I think sometimes we really believe that if Jesus came to this earth today that He would join us.

And we cannot escape the conclusion that one of the main reasons the hierarchy of Jerusalem did not accept Jesus was because they could not accept His leadership. He was hobnobbing with common people, catering to the sick and infirm, the poor and disfigured, women and children. They did not want to be part of any organization, any kingdom, that expected its leaders to bend to others like that.

Jesus announced that His ministry and kingdom would be focused on the poor and oppressed, prisoners, and profligates. His interpretation of Messiah-ship was totally foreign to everything they understood, taught, believed or practiced. When they saw what Jesus' intentions were, they determined that He could not be their Messiah. They rejected Him as their Savior and recognized Him as a threat to everything they believed and practiced, including their system of leadership.

For the One

Of hens and chicks

Jesus used a powerful metaphor to reveal how absurd it is for us to expect Him to follow us. With painful haunting words, He cried out—voice choking—"O Jerusalem, Jerusalem, the city that kills the prophets and stones those who are sent to it! How often would I have gathered your children together as a hen gathers her brood under her wings, and you were not willing" (Matthew 23:37).

There is so much here to consider. His words reveal that Jesus is trying to gather us even in the midst of our rebellion. While we are stoning and killing His prophets and messengers, Jesus is still trying to gather us. He does not wait for us to change our ways. He tries to gather us in the midst of our stubbornness and our recalcitrance. "While are yet sinners"—that's how much He loves us.

But Jesus used very specific language, describing the people as "children" and "chicks."

We might think it is our church. We might believe we are in charge of it. But Jesus says it is His. And the "test of fellowship" is not the religious rituals that they—and we—might obsess about. It isn't about how we tithe or keep the Sabbath. All of those things are superficial in comparison with the weightier matter of Whom we have submitted our lives to.

Think about the contrast He was making here. Jesus gave this stinging rebuke of their leadership, then He tells them how He views them. They are "chicks"—little babies newly hatched from their eggs.

Do you understand the condition of chicks when they are born? How dependent they are on the mother hen?

Hens do the birthing, the bathing, the feeding, the protecting, not the chicks. Hens do everything; the chicks do nothing. They can't even see when they're newly hatched. The chick depends totally and completely on the mother hen for everything. They contribute nothing to the process. If the hen leaves her chicks, they will not survive. And—in a sense—the hen does not need the chicks. If she loses all of them, she can lay more eggs and a few weeks later will have a new brood.

"Jesus. All." is not just some slogan. It is how this whole thing works between us and God. He is everything, all of it.

There is no such thing as "Jesus And" with hens and chicks—as if there's something that the chick can contribute to the relationship. If a chick contributes nothing for his or her survival in the relationship to their mother hen, why do we think we have something to contribute in our relationship with Jesus? Why are we so self-important, thinking we're so indispensable? In your relationship with Jesus, who is gathering whom?

The hen is the perfect example of a servant leader. In the relationship between the hen and her chicks, the chicks don't serve the hen. It's always the hen who serves the chicks. And if she does not serve them, the chicks will die. She serves selflessly, and will give her life to protect and save her chicks.

So why is it that we chicks are always trying to direct Jesus? Using Jesus' metaphor, the notion that chicks could lead the hen or tell the hen what to do is utterly ridiculous. Yet that's how many of us relate to Jesus every day, in our personal lives and in our church lives.

But, in spite of us, Jesus will keep trying to gather us.

The Jesus question

And here's the reason that rejecting servant leadership is so dangerous. If we reject Christ's leadership and fail to practice it, we will eventually reject Jesus. And not just reject Him, ultimately we will crucify Him. Jesus becomes an enemy to us that we cannot allow to remain alive. If we don't die to self, we will eventually kill the Savior.

And here's the kicker: Every day at the end of the temple sacrifices—during the time of Jesus—the final sacrifice that the priest offered was a sacrifice for the emperor of Rome. It was a symbol of their allegiance to him.

In John 19:15, when Pilate asked the people, "Shall I crucify your king?" The Bible says that the priest and religious leaders answered Pilate, "We have no king but Caesar!"

After we reject and crucify Jesus, we will always put another king in His place. So who are you making your sacrifices to at the end of your day? Whose leadership are you aligned with?

For the One

"Jesus. All." is not some slogan, or a fad, or phase we're going through. It is the perennial and urgent question for each of us and for all of us as a church.

Matthew 23 ends with this sorrowful invitation of Jesus, a metaphor of hens and chicks that demonstrated the love and leadership of God. In the next chapter (Matthew 24), prompted by His disciples, Jesus was talking about the destruction of Jerusalem, the end of the world and the second coming of Christ. In this sequence, time is running out for the church—so what are you going to do with Jesus?

Can you accept your role as a chick? Or do you still have to be in charge?

---

1. Ellen White, *Testimonies for the Church, Volume 1*, page 166.

Cross-shaped Faith

Jesus in our experience

Terry Swenson

I spent years running around trying to find out what church was. But as I got busier and busier, I felt emptier and emptier, and more and more frustrated.

I came to the realization it wasn't just me. Too many of my generation are not here in the church today. They're gone. They became burned out and disillusioned or found a place to run to and hide from the storm.

We are told repeatedly that "We are the church"—or "You are the church." But is that the fact in real time? When I was taught how to be a pastor, we were told that we were to get people to realize that it's about them, it's about the system. We work on getting them to come to the worship service, support the appropriate programs, get into small groups, go tell others, and pretty soon the church building fills up to capacity. A full house means a successful church.

But a wrong concept doesn't become right by repetition. Because, if the church is about me, it's not going to work! I'm not big enough. The church is about—must be about—something and Someone much bigger. It's about Jesus Christ.

Re-reading a familiar chapter

I've searched for a long time to put my finger on what's going on. More and more we hear voices telling us what is and what is not, and who is and who is not. But what pulled it all together for me was the great theologian Paul. It's in the chapter we all enjoy talking about—1 Corinthians 13.

"Oh yeah," I hear you say. "The love chapter. There he goes, the love

For the One

guy always talking about love. When do we get to the meaty parts of our theology?"

But it was within this chapter that I had read so many times in my life that clarity came to me. Paul is speaking to us, to this church, today. Paul is *describing* to us what the church should be all about in the eyes of Jesus:

> If I speak in the tongues of men or of angels, but do not have love, I am only a resounding gong or a clanging cymbal. If I have the gift of prophecy and can fathom all mysteries and all knowledge, and if I have a faith that can move mountains, but do not have love, I am nothing. If I give all I possess to the poor and give over my body to hardship that I may boast, but do not have love, I gain nothing (1 Corinthians 13:1–3, NIV).

Did you catch the delineations Paul makes here? Let me tell it to you in a different way—the way it jumped off the page to me.

If I can speak—or sing—in all the languages of earth and of angels; if I am the best speaker in the world and can use words so glorious that people said, "This is not a man, but an angel of God speaking!"; if I have people flocking to whatever building I am in; but if I don't love others, I am just a bunch of irritating noise.

If I have the gift of prophecy, if I am so good that I know God's secret plans; if I can line it out so we know everything; if I have that kind of prophetic gift but I don't have love, I am nothing.

If I am the greatest academic of the world and possess all knowledge; if I know Greek, Hebrew, Aramaic, and can make up languages and make you think they were real; if I have degrees so long that you can't even fit them on a bulletin; yet if I don't have love, I am nothing.

If I give everything I have to the poor; if I am the world's greatest proponent of social justice; if people had me on Oprah and they renamed all of the Martin Luther King Boulevards after Terry Swenson; if they forget about Gandhi and called *me* Terry G; yet if I don't have love, I am nothing.

Paul goes on: "If I have faith that can move mountains . . ."

Who said that in the Bible? Paul is quoting the words of Jesus—so even if I fulfil the words of Jesus Himself, where I actually have that faith as a mustard seed; and that mountain goes flying into orbit, and everybody's like "Whoa, you are a man of God!"; yet if I don't love, I am nothing!

What Paul understood was this: it's not about me. It's about Jesus. It's about Jesus' love. It's about Jesus' love lived out through us.

Paul realized something else about all these other things: without love all things build up walls. Walls are frightening things, built because of fear and, sometimes, built to propagate fear.

Without walls

At Loma Linda University where I minister, at least 50 per cent of our students aren't Adventist. They ask me questions that cause me to re-examine the Word of God. Prompted by one such question recently, I was looking at the Bible trying to see it in a fresh way, and the thought occurred to me, "Why did they kill Jesus?"

It was because He said He was the Messiah, right? I don't think so. There were hundreds of messiahs running around. They didn't kill Jesus because he was Messiah.

Well then, if it was not because of His claims of Messiah-ship, what was it about Jesus that united the Pharisees and the Sadducees, the polar extremes that hated each other, along with Herod's followers and Rome? What was it that brought four disparate powers together against this common man from Nazareth?

> What Paul understood was this: it's not about me. It's about Jesus. It's about Jesus' love.

And then it hit me.

When Jesus was about to be crucified, Pilate had Him scourged and brought out to the judgment hall. Pilate addressed the crowd and said, "Every Passover I give you a choice—and I'm going to let you pick again. Do you want Jesus, or do you want Barabbas?"

Pilot gave them a choice: "Do you want this son of God—Barabbas—or the Son of God—Jesus? This guy, Jesus, is kinda mellow and I kinda like him, and this dude, Barrabas, is a terrorist—he's crazy. Which one do you want?"

For the One

In my estimation, they didn't crucify Jesus Christ because He said He was the Messiah. They crucified Jesus because all four of those power entities said, "You hear what this guy says? In His kingdom there are no walls. How do you have power without walls? How do you have power without fear? How do you have power without control? We have to kill this man! He's messing up all of our games. We can squabble about who's got the walls, who's the biggest and baddest walls, but, if we don't get rid of Him, *we* won't have any walls."

How do I know that? I return to reading Paul again.

Galatians 3:27, 28 declares that Jesus' kingdom is about destroying walls. It says that all who have been united with Jesus Christ in baptism have put on Christ like putting on new clothes—they're covered with Jesus. There is no longer Jew or Gentile, slave or free, male or female, we are all in Christ Jesus. There is no longer people who are in and out, there are no more racial, national or cultural distinctions, no socio-economic status, and no more gender discrimination. We are all one. Paul got what Jesus lived and proclaimed.

Two things

When I search scripture, I only find one place where it says Jesus built any kind of walls:

> As you come to him, the living Stone—rejected by humans but chosen by God and precious to him—you also, like living stones, are being built into a spiritual house to be a holy priesthood, offering spiritual sacrifices acceptable to God through Jesus Christ (1 Peter 2:4, 5, NIV).

In construction, when you lay bricks, that first one is the most important. You take a lot of time on that first brick. You string a line, and you align all your other bricks off it. Jesus is that first all-important brick. Jesus sets the line; He's the key to it all. And He says, "I'm going to mortar you together as living stones, and the walls I build with you will become the temple and shrine of who I am."

He's saying that we are the intersection between God and humanity. In Matthew 22:37–40, Jesus showed us how we become that living temple, how we can be filled with the presence of Christ. Responding to the question, "What's the greatest thing out there?"—He said, "Love the

Lord your God with all your heart and with all your soul and with all your mind. This is the first and greatest commandment." And He said that the second is equally important: "Love your neighbor as yourself."

But perhaps the most startling statement is in the next verse, where He said, "All the Law and the Prophets hang on these two commandments." He was talking about what we know as the Old Testament—the Scriptures. Jesus said, "You want to know what is most important? It's not the hundreds and hundreds of things from the Talmud. It's not even the 10 things from Mount Sinai. I'll boil it down for you. The whole universe bases itself on these two things. And if you get that right, you will have the experience that I'm talking about."

Cross-shaped construction

If I were to give a symbol for this, it would look like a cross.

The first thing Jesus is talking about is the vertical beam of the cross—the relationship between God and you. Jesus says, "If you've seen me, you've seen the Father" (see John 14:9). How Jesus viewed and acted toward people, that's exactly how God views you.

I am loved, forgiven and made whole, but I don't deserve forgiveness. I never get to a point where I can say, "Jesus, you can go away now because I've got it, I'm OK now." When He shows me again and again how much He loves me—that's a start.

> I never get to a point where I can say, "Jesus, you can go away now because I've got it, I'm OK now."

But, in Jesus' kingdom, that's not enough. We've been saying that's enough, but it is not. If all you have is a single beam relationship it become a stick. Unfortunately, some people will take that and use it as a stick to beat people with.

Jesus said the second command is loving others, and loving yourself. God created us to be relational beings—just look at Genesis 1. The only thing God said wasn't good that He had made was men existing alone. The world became perfect when women were made and intimate relational community was formed!

For the One

But neither is it enough to have only horizontal relationships, because these are relationships without boundaries. Left to ourselves we create all kinds of combinations of relationships, all kinds of physical interactions, all kinds of brokenness and emptiness because people don't have the guidelines that God set up for His kingdom or relationships.

Just one beam is emptiness; but where those two beams intersect, you have the crosshairs of the kingdom that targets the community Christ created us for.

Starting now

A reference that always caught my attention when I was younger was the description of Adam and Eve in Genesis 2:25: "And they were both naked, the man and his wife, and were not ashamed." After I got past the distraction, I wondered why that was in the story.

It was then I noticed that when sin entered the world and the connection with Jesus Christ was broken, the first thing we did was realize we were naked. We covered ourselves. When that wasn't enough, we hid. And we've been covering and hiding ever since.

Wouldn't you like to go back to Eden again? A place where you can be open? A place where you can be vulnerable? A place where you can share your hurts? A place where you can trust others?

It is not going to happen with just one beam or the other—but when you put them together, when you understand what Jesus Christ did for you and how He feels, you can create that world once again. You can forgive the unforgivable. You can trust when you've been broken and hurt. You can be a circle of belonging; a circle that isn't exclusive.

Remember, that's what people hated about Jesus. He couldn't get the exclusiveness thing right according to how they defined it. Even His disciples said, "Not them, Jesus—us!" But Jesus kept drawing the circle bigger and saying, "Come in, come in! I love you. Come in, you are forgiven. Come in and experience heaven. Come in."

Could it be that we can tear down the walls?

I don't want to fight the battles anymore. I'm tired of seeing members, beautiful people, powerful leaders, crash and burn and die inside. I'm tired of tasting honey that turns to ashes in my mouth. It's about Jesus.

Jesus in Our Practice

All. If people want to march around saying "*We* are the church!" then that's OK. But I'm a follower of Jesus.

It's about Jesus. We can have the kind of life He created us to experience. Because what transforms us is the realization of His love lifted up for us. It has changed me. I have tasted something glorious, and I want you to taste it, too.

I think of Joel 2:28 where it says, "Then, after doing all those things, I will pour out my Spirit upon all people. Your sons and daughters will prophesy. Your old men will dream dreams, and your young men will see visions."

Have you dreamed lately? Do you see those visions? Or are you scarred and battered from the war? That's alright. Jesus knows. And He's going do something about it—starting now.

Trusting God, Washing Feet

Jesus and practicing reconciliation

Lisa Clark Diller

I have hated someone. Not a big epic hatred, but the most sinister kind of mundane, ugly, ordinary, and small hatred. It's a juicy story, but I am not going to get distracted with the details here. There are no innocent people in this story, though I definitely felt justified in my loathing.

It was the kind of feeling where my skin crawled if I had to be in the same room with the person. I got angry and felt like crying when anyone said anything good about them. My hatred took up all my emotional energy. I thought and talked more about the situation than it ever deserved.

And most corrosively, I held on to the hatred even though, on my knees before God, I knew it kept me from fully entering the kingdom of God. I actually would say to God in prayer, "God, I know I will not enter into the New Earth with this hatred—and I just don't care."

I didn't want to change my feelings—and I didn't *want* to want to change. There seemed to be no space for normalcy, for restored relationship.

Jesus in Our Practice

Public reconciliation

But there are happier stories about hate changing to forgiveness, stories of reconciliation. In June 2013, the British government formally apologized to the Kikuyu people of Kenya for the torture and other horrific abuses they had received at the hands of the colonial government in the 1950s. Almost 200 elderly Kikuyu people traveled to sit before the British high commissioner in Nairobi to receive the apology. On behalf of the British government, he expressed "sincere regret" that these abuses had taken place, announced payments of £2600 to each of 5200 claimants, and urged that the process of healing for both nations begin.

Most of the survivors echoed the sentiments of 82-year-old Wamutwe Ngau, who was tortured and mutilated so badly that he was unable to have children. He said, "In my culture, if someone says they are sorry, you have to accept it." For him, the apology was worth much more than the little money that was offered.

Of course, other countries have also done this sort of thing. Australia's National Sorry Day in 2008 called attention to this kind of national attempt to come to grips with past injustice. In the United States, it took until the 1990s for the government to officially apologize for legalizing racial slavery.

But in such situations, who has the harder part—the person being forgiven or the person forgiving? They are both really challenging situations to be in. There are historical circumstances, reasons why people behaved badly. In the Kenyan situation, neither the prime minister nor the high commissioner representing Great Britain had themselves participated in these atrocities. Why should they apologize?

The entire situation begs the question: How does reconciliation happen in these and other, perhaps less-visible, less-public circumstances? When there has been pain and betrayal, how do people start again and work to build the Kingdom together?

The Jesus model

I think Jesus modeled one of the primary ways we can do this in the footwashing story, narrated in its larger context in John 12:44–13:14.

First, He claimed He reveals God. And the best way to reveal God is to

For the One

emphasize God's love for the humans He created. More than that, Jesus is Himself God. This is a huge claim, but Jesus' security in who He was enabled Him to move forward with the rest of His actions here. As His disciples, we also can be secure in who we are—in Whose we are—and that should be the foundation for all that we do.

Second, Jesus showed God's love through what He *did*. He did this tangibly, physically, by washing the feet of His disciples. The text says that this is the "full extent of his love" (John 13:1, NLT). I don't know why Jesus did this particular act, but the text says He did it with a full awareness of His power. And He not only did what a servant would have done, but what a *female* servant usually did. This was women's work.

The Gospel of John is full of expressions of Jesus as mother/woman, and His willingness to tell His male disciples to act as women in washing feet was really powerful and upsetting. You can see how outraged and confused the disciples were in this passage. Jesus was asking them to violate all sorts of social norms. So Jesus showed the full extent of His love, by acting counter-culturally—radically—in order to serve and fully identify with those at the bottom of the power systems. He knew that asking His disciples to do this would mean making them think differently about those weaker people.

Next, Jesus said He did what He did without judgment. When Jesus modeled unity and reconciliation, He turned upside down all the concerns about who was right and who was wrong. His disciples had spent a lot of the previous days wracked by conflict and jealousy. Jesus hadn't done something wrong that He needed to apologize for, but He acted as a servant because He wanted to move the ego-boosting conversation about position and policy-making out of the way—it is hard to talk about that when you're busy washing each other's feet.

And look at the statements Jesus makes about what He was doing. Fascinatingly, He says He was not to judge the world (see John 12:47). There is judgment—but Jesus distanced Himself from that. He trusted His Father and encouraged us to do the same. This is about a revelation of love and a bringing together of God and humanity. His concern was with the saving/serving, not the judgment/losing part. He let that take care of itself.

I'm not saying that people are to submit to abusers and participate in the empowerment of evil. But the peace, forgiveness, and reconciliation that we are called to as God's children is more often challenged by our own hurt feelings and self-justification than it is by true victimization. I believe and hope that communion- and service-based peacemaking will clear the way for resistance to evil in all its forms.

Finally—and most importantly for us here today—we see that Jesus asked us to do the same thing He did. We are His representatives and we are to act as He did in the world. The meal and deeds described in John 13 have remained the most sacred acts that Christians participate in.

Practicing Communion

In our tradition, we call this Communion. It is how, historically and into the present, the church enacted its commitment to reconciliation, to being followers of Jesus, to participating and acknowledging the Incarnation. It was weird then—and it is weird now. It requires that we act out, in our bodies, our ideas about God's love becoming flesh, about service and identification with the poor and downtrodden. We do it in such an odd and radical way that no-one can mistake what we are doing for anything other than what we have declared it to symbolize. We aren't going to accidentally do something like this. And there is no such thing as a "mere" symbol—when we do something, we make it real.

> It requires that we act out, in our bodies, our ideas about God's love becoming flesh.

Participating in communion also requires other people—other people who might be messed up, might not totally believe the right way, might not always live the right way. In order to be part of this most identifying act within Christianity, we have to suspend some of our judgment of the other people around us.

If we practice foot-washing, we see that we are to take the parts of the person who is the one extending forgiveness *and* the one being forgiven. Have you noticed this? It is very telling. We all might like to play the part of Jesus—we want to be the magnanimous one, the person reaching out. But sometimes we are the ones who need forgiving. And more to the point, it isn't our job to tell the difference all the time, so in foot-washing, we play both parts.

Part of what is sad about the way the church has split apart over the centuries is that we stopped taking Communion together. We developed different branches of Christianity because people didn't want to do Communion together. But if we can't even be in communion, we won't ever be reconciled. So often this ceremony has been a divider—a way of showing who was in and who was not. It was something to aspire to and revealed who was a mature and fully-fledged member.

We have even split the church by gender for Communion, although the early church never did this. In fact, Greeks and Romans around the early Christians accused them of sexual immorality because the men and women worshipped and celebrated Communion together. The church adopted this sexualization of foot-washing, forgetting that Jesus crossed class and gender lines to do something a woman would have done and which scandalized His disciples.

Instead, we need to embrace the acts of Communion as emblematic of how God wants us to be together. Sometimes participating in these acts creates the space where we can actually love and bond with each other. We can practice being the Body of Christ to each other.

What if Communion became a time of radical boundary crossing for service to others? What if we were able to focus on that to the extent that we embraced the humility and weirdness and physicality *in order* to say that service, love and giving/receiving forgiveness are central to following Jesus? Communion could become the ordinary, regular way in which we show up for worship and ministry, crossing boundaries to bond with those we have challenges with, serving each other and enacting the truth that we are both forgiving and forgiven.

Living Communion

In so doing, we must go beyond the symbolic reminder to living out the ideals in practice. As Jesus did, we will start with knowing who we and our fellow humans are in relation to God. Jesus told the disciples that they were clean, they were saved. The foot-washing wasn't about saving them—the serving was icing on the cake, giving them tangible, physical reminders of who they were before God, and of who they were to be to each other. This wasn't about salvation, it was about receiving the blessing of being the beloved of God. Like Jesus, we trust God to take care of the details and the judgment.

This leads to reconciliation between and among us because in our service we are not trying to save someone so we can check that off our list. We do this because we both love and are loved, and we want to show love to others. We want to identify with all God's children, especially the least of these. We participate in acts—of service, of identification—even before we understand why or how they are important. Maybe we go though several levels of understanding in our spiritual walk, in our service. We might serve people, and be served, without knowing what is being done.

And this isn't a mere intellectual or symbolic exercise. I think Jesus asked His disciples to practice this because He didn't want it to be a verbal metaphor, the way "servant leadership" can so often be. We become the Body of Jesus in the world through actual, physical, practical service—with, and for, each other.

So we wash the feet of the world, but only after we have practiced this with each other. Don't run away to the exotic land of serving the poor and working for justice together, without also committing to regularly worshipping with the Body of Christ, practicing and enacting forgiveness with each other in the Christian church. I think Jesus asked us to meet together to act out our commitment to the incarnation because He knew we needed to be in each other's presence, to show up regularly together in order to practice loving.

> We participate in acts—of service, of identification—even before we understand why or how they are important.

Practicing miracles

My friend Melissa gave me some good advice that reflects some of these kingdom values. She said she had a person in her life she just loathed. This person irritated the life out of her. But she said she would

For the One

practice standing near that person. Not necessarily talking to them, just practicing being near them. And it helped. She gradually saw them for the human they were, rather than the annoying object in her life.

For my hatred—sordid, miserable little drama that it was—I was sort of willing to put myself in a position where God could change me. This meant not running from the other person. We ended up spending the better part of a summer in close proximity, doing mundane tasks like work and life together.

I don't know when or how it happened, but at the end of the summer, I didn't have any more hate. It remains one of the biggest miracles of my life, that imperceptible shift away from toxic hate to mutual living, mutual service, the seeing of the other as an ordinary human like myself. But it happened because of proximity and serving together. This transformation of my own heart without me doing anything overt—just letting God do His thing, while I did my thing—might be small compared to the things you've seen God do, but it is a tangible work of God for me.

In the years since, I have also had to realize, as in the story of the Good Samaritan, that I am on the receiving end of service. I have sometimes had my feet and wounds washed by people who I think are profoundly wrong.

But am I ready to receive that service? What kind of peace and reconciliation happen when I receive the help of someone who is sexist or racist, or someone I think is wrong about how we should organize our church? Can I accept the love and service of those whose ideas and beliefs I find laughable or abhorrent?

I believe this is what Jesus is asking of me—of us. And it can start in our worship and Communion together.

Trusting God, washing feet, building the peaceable kingdom.

Living Jesus

Jesus and our ministry

Eddie Hypolite

I am Christianity. I don't want to be seen as some spiritual contradiction or a type of Adventist anomaly. I don't want to push against the tides just because I can. I am misunderstood, maybe. But I am not confused.

I am Christianity. View me through the wide angles of dissent or the magnified image under criticism, but I am still Christianity. People read the story of Christ in the Bible and see it played out in my life. They understand the Christ that I love in the attention that I pay them. They see, in me, the drama of His life played out in real-time. They see the nakedness of my humanity fused with the indefinable divine life that somehow makes sense to them.

I am Christianity. My life is growing in the midst of victory and defeat. The perfection that I crave, He gives me. And the perfection He gives me for living is perfect faith and perfect obedience. It's weird because sometimes, things don't make sense to me until I have trusted and obeyed Him—and then ding!

I am Christianity. I am Christianity because Jesus has invested life and blood in me.

I am Christianity because He says that I am inextricably linked to Him. He chooses to be linked to me in the same way.

I am Christianity despite who I am in my daily grind and my private madness. He is not ashamed of me. He calls me brother, even friend. My faith isn't based on the life of a dead philosopher. It is affirmed by the life of a living God: Jesus Christ. Because He lives, my life grows. My continued life in Him and His continued life in me somehow makes sense. He touches the dead places around me and gives me life.

I am Christianity. I am not trying to be anything else. I am Christianity

For the One

without apology. You will never feel uncomfortable around me just because you are not a Christian. If people didn't feel that way around Jesus, then who am I—who is called "Christian"—to make you feel that way? Take me or leave me. Love me or hate me. But no matter what you do with me—or how you do it—know that when you meet me, I am Christianity.

His mission identity

I have spent most of my ministerial career so far doing urban ministry. It has been a dream doing ministry among varied people groups in London, the city of my birth and re-birth.

I jokingly say that Jesus gave me two bridges that allow me to travel "undetected" between our church community and the non-churched community and visa-versa. The result is a broadened view of society that is sometimes missed when only ministering to the church community.

My life and ministry over the past few years have been turning toward understanding that Jesus is the center of who I truly am and who we are. He is the center of everything we do, the whole and only conversation worth having. I'm consumed with Christ and His mission, and its implication to all we are and do.

I want to look at the way Jesus did mission. In Isaiah 61:1, 2, we read:

> The Spirit of the Lord God is upon me, because the Lord has anointed me to bring good news to the poor; he has sent me to bind up the brokenhearted, to proclaim liberty to the captives, and the opening of the prison to those who are bound; to proclaim the year of the Lord's favor.

Hundreds of years later, a young Rabbi stood up in His hometown, opened the scrolls of Isaiah, and pronounced this verse to the world. Then when John's disciples came to Jesus because an imprisoned John wished to know if Jesus is truly the One, what did Jesus do? He told them to spend a couple of days with Him, after which time He sent them back to John with the message, "Go and tell John what you have seen and heard: the blind receive their sight, the lame walk, lepers are cleansed, and the deaf hear, the dead are raised up, the poor have good news preached to them" (Luke 7:22).

This expected-but-unexpected Jesus was someone no-one expected

Jesus in Our Practice

Him to be. But look at the prior echoes of this same Lord. In Exodus 3, He remembered a promise He made to Abraham and Isaac and Jacob. Hundreds of years later, He spoke to an 80-year-old fugitive from a burning bush: "I have surely seen the affliction of my people who are in Egypt and have heard their cry because of their taskmasters. I know their sufferings, and I have come down to deliver them out of the hand of the Egyptians" (Exodus 3:7, 8).

Wow, just listen to how He speaks! He speaks with this Exodus yearning, prior to His incarnated entrance into the human story, then He speaks in this familiar way once He gets here. And why does He do so? He does this so that when the incarnated Lord speaks we will know who He is. He knows that if we know who He is, then we begin to truly know who we are. He speaks this way also, so that we can see His divine intentionality: He sees, He hears, He knows, He responds, and He comes. The Lord has seen, the Lord has heard, the Lord knows, and He is responding.

He was announcing to the world what type of Savior He is. He was announcing to the world what type of Messiah He is. He was announcing to the world what type of mission He has so that when we see it, we will recognize it.

> **He does this so that when the incarnated Lord speaks we will know who He is.**

In Genesis 1, we see that divine intentionality. We've seen this divine intentionality through the church. We've seen it consistently. Jesus said that if we have seen Him do, we are to do likewise.

We know that the church doesn't exist unto itself. It is not some private club. Voices come and voices go—but God is God. We come and we go—but God still is. But when we look to Jesus, we see this divine intentionality. And we begin to see what our mission should look like, in light of His mission: Jesus was proactive, community-centered, and relationally intentional. He responded through His ministry, the ministry of His disciples, the apostles, and the church—if it, too, is proactive, community-centered, and relationally intentional.

For the One

Proactive

Christian proactivity is about the actions of Christ, not the endless debate about Christ. But—for me—the most important question is: How do I portray this Christ to others? How do I minister this Christ to the world?

When I go back to London, how do I minister this Christ? When I go to my sauna where there are people with names like "Turkish Ed," "Terry the Talker," and "Davie Wolf," how do I minister this Christ?

For us as a church, this is a constant struggle.

We must intentionally find the lost and hurting in humanity, as Jesus intentionally found us. They're all around us. We must see as He saw. We must hear as He heard. We must know as He knew. And we must respond as He responded. That's what Jesus did throughout scripture. That's what Jesus does throughout history. He sees us—"I've seen you. Go and sin no more" (see John 8:10, 11). He hears us. He knows—"I know he isn't your man. And the men you were with before weren't yours either" (see John 4:17, 18). He responds—"Father forgive them, for they know not what they've done" (see Luke 23:34). This is our mission. This is our action. This is what the Lord has asked us to do.

I was running a basketball ministry at the church I pastored in south London. We were doing a basketball camp in the projects. I was sitting on a wall, and just behind me there was a group of kids arguing. There was this one little girl—about 10 years old—and she went off. Every other word was a "BEEP this" and "BEEP that."

And I thought, *Well, who the BEEP is that?*—and I did say, "BEEP" in my head. I turned to the girl and I said, "What's wrong with you and your little dirty-mouth speaking? Do better than that."

There was a boy named Demetrius, whom I knew, sitting next to her. So I waved at him. And her friend was looking at me kind of intimidatingly.

I looked back at Demetrius and I heard the girl who was looking at me fiercely ask him who I was.

"That's Pastor Eddie," he said

"Are you kidding?" she replied. "Don't lie about him being a pastor."

"I'm serious—he's a pastor," he answered.

But she still didn't believe him. So he told her to go and ask me, if she didn't believe him.

So she got up and came over to me, now more curious than fierce. "Excuse me, are you a pastor?"

"Yes, I am a pastor," I told her.

"Don't mess around with me. Are you really a pastor?" she asked again.

"What's wrong? Don't I look like a pastor?"

"No—for real, are you a pastor?"

"Honestly, darling, I'm a pastor," I assured her.

Then she turned it around, "Will you bless me?"

This time, I asked her if she was serious.

She told me that she was, so I put my hand on her head and asked her what her name was. It sounded like "Flower," so I said simply, "Lord, bless Flower."

Immediately, Demetrius stood up. He said, "Well, if you're going to bless her, then you're going to bless me, pastor."

I ended up "blessing" about eight kids at the park that afternoon. I was still sitting on the wall. And the little girl who had been cussing came to me and asked me to bless her too.

"You were the girl who was just cussing up the place, weren't you?" I asked her.

"I know, but would you bless me anyway?"

And I blessed her, too.

The world wants to be blessed. They want to be blessed by the Christ that resides in us. They want to be blessed by the life of Christ.

Be proactive.

Community-centered

We must also be community-centered—and that is community-centered in two ways: the internal community and the external community.

The book of Ephesians is the great book of the New Testament because for the first time Paul stands up and says that this is who we are as Christians. The Lord has created an alternative humanity. He says

For the One

this is who we are. This is our identity. This life with Christ in us creates a new community. If we believe in this high Christology, this affects the way I live with you. I cannot be one with Christ and "two" with you. I can't sit at the welcome table without you, and you can't sit at the table without me.

I am the youngest of 10 children. In my house, there was no "Hypolite referendum" on whether or not my parents would have children. They just had them and said, "This is your brother and your sister. Know them. Love them." That was how it was from child 1 to child 10.

Just as there was no Hypolite referendum, there is no referendum with God either. There is no human committee that decides who is born of the Spirit and who is not. We need to focus on giving thanks that we are here personally. And so we build the community. We need to think about the way we build the internal community, because we are the alternative community.

Then there is the external community. In Luke 4:18, Jesus is modeling salvation extended to the poor, the prisoners, the blind, and the oppressed.

We need a community that centers itself in its "Jesus identity," while also celebrating His life and teachings. Christ is my identity; Adventism is my theology. And it's a great marriage because I share my life with society; everything else is just a Bible study.

If you want to know what Jesus is like, just come into my house. Come meet my family. We need a community that is Jesus-centered.

In Europe we have to begin from scratch with the teaching of Jesus Christ. People hear "Jesus Christ" and they think it's an expletive, because that's the only context they hear His name in. We have so completely removed Jesus from the minds and lives of society. They don't know that Jesus is the reason they get up every morning. They don't understand that He is the reason they have food and clothes. They don't even know that He is actively seeking to make Himself known to them.

So we find ourselves with our Christ identity, seeking to grow as a community internally and externally, by simply sharing this Christ life with anyone and everyone.

Awhile back, I was running one of my social education workshops, called "How to Be a Player," in West London where I grew up. One Friday night, I was talking to the kids beforehand and I met a kid named Frank. I asked him where he lived and how he had been enjoying the workshop.

"Oh, it was alright," he said. "At first, I was only coming out for the prizes, but then I really got into it, you know?"

So I asked him, "Did it make sense?"

"No," he said. "You made sense."

My heart sort of jumped, and the light bulb went on in my head. The community has to make sense. People are hearing "sense" all the time. You want to know what sense means? Just type "sense" into Google, and you'll get 20 million hits. But Jesus truly made sense. Why? What He said and who He was were one and the same. There was no contradiction.

That's what people want. They want a community that makes sense.

And that's what I want. I want to be that person who makes sense. I want what I speak and who I am to be one and the same.

That was Jesus' mission. That's the way in which Jesus revealed the Father.

Relationally intentional

Does my faith draw other people to me and—more importantly—to Jesus? John said it this way: "That which we have seen and heard we proclaim also to you, so that you too may have fellowship with us; and indeed our fellowship is with the Father and with his Son Jesus Christ" (1 John 1:3). Christianity is a lived experience that should affect both the church and society. Too often, our kids are raised to love church and, hopefully, they find Jesus later on, but I want our kids to be raised to know Jesus.

I am already thinking about the church that my daughter has to grow up in. And I want her to grow up in a church where she grows to know Him. She's growing in a home where she's growing to know Jesus. And believe me, she loves her Jesus, the way she talks about Him and celebrates Him. It's a wonderful thing to see. And that's what I want to see in our church as well.

> Just type "sense" into Google, and you'll get 20 million hits. But Jesus truly made sense.

For the One

With this "Jesus life" in us, Jesus wants to draw people to us. Because if they have met me, then the have met Him; not in any way that we think we are God, but in a way that His life is linked to my life. Jesus wants that to be our lived experience because Jesus was relationally intentional. He always has been.

This is His desire for the church. Does my faith draw people to me and to Jesus? Does my community draw people to Jesus? This is what I want my church to be. I want people to want to be around our people. They don't even know Jesus, but they want to be around us. And—by extension—around Jesus.

There was a young man named Nathan who came to a camp that we ran called "Community Camp" to which anybody from the community could come. Other than the staff, everyone is non-Adventist. It is a wonderful thing to see.

At the camps, we were talking about Jesus and this young girl went up to Nathan and said, "Nathan, do you believe all this Jesus stuff they're talking about? Do you believe in it?"

I love his reply: "Yeah, when I'm around these people, I believe in Jesus."

It didn't take any Bible studies, no evangelistic meetings, no 28 Fundamental Beliefs, and no great writings from a prophet—just "When I am around them, yeah, I believe in Jesus."

That was all: relationally intentional. That's Jesus' desire for us.

So what is the "Jesus way" then? Jesus meets the primary needs of the people. Jesus gains the respect of the people. Jesus earns the trust of the people. Jesus saves the people. Jesus says to us, "Go, therefore, and do likewise."

We have to go out and know the needs of people. We need to win the respect of the people and earn their trust. And we can help save the people. That is the life of Jesus in community. That's the Jesus way.

"Thy Kingdom Come"

Living Jesus' kingdom today

Joanna Darby

I recently overheard my boys—aged five and three—"packing bags" in their room. I was curious. We had no trips away planned anytime soon, but I didn't inquire until later, when I heard them again chatting about what they had packed.

"So what did you pack?"

"Lego."

"What for?"

"For heaven."

"Why?"

"So we're ready."

"Ready for what?"

"For heaven. That's what heaven is. Lots of Lego."

For a moment, I considered explaining that there might not *actually* be Lego in heaven . . .

But then I remembered the devastation I had felt when my teachers and parents had been telling me for years that heaven was the most fun exciting wonderful place you can imagine—which in a kid's brain is obviously "Disneyland with chocolate rivers and giant slippery slides and cake for breakfast and riding bikes all night"—and then, all of a

For the One

sudden, we were told the "truth." We would all work in a garden. Every day. For eternity.

Do you remember that bizarre transition? At one point, it was OK to think that heaven was like a fun park but then you were told this "truth"—that heaven was more like a farming work camp.

So as I considered how to explain to my five year old that heaven is really more about peace and rest, I realized that for a mother, Lego really is peace and rest. Hours of peace and rest in a bucket of colored plastic snap-locking pieces. So maybe Jasper is right. Maybe heaven is Lego.

Are we there yet?

We know so little about heaven. We are certain of it and it's wonder and glory, but we really don't know what it will be like. Or how it will all happen. For all of the prophecies and charts and diagrams with funny arches, we really don't know.

I know it is our great message to look forward to Christ's return. But are we just waiting? Is this life just about waiting around to be with Jesus? Is this whole world just a queue?

That's not an inspiring message. I mean, the heaven thing is *nice*. But not only is that not very useful to me now, but that sounds a bit like a selfish consumerist Christianity. Is this all salvation is? Getting to heaven? And is everything good on hold until then?

The result of this kind of "earth to heaven trajectory" is that we can sit in our churches and become like kids in the back seat whining, "Are we there yet? Are we there yet? Are we there yet? Mom, he won't share. His leg is on my side. I'm bored. Are we there yet? I feel sick. I'm hungry. Are we there yet? . . ."

All we want to do is leave here and get there. All our energy, attention and focus—and much of our teaching and church budget—is directed down this one-way street: getting to heaven and getting others to heaven. When what God actually gives us is something entirely different—and entirely more exciting.

Jesus in Our Practice

Heaven to earth

The Son of God has been *earthed* into our humanity for all time. In *Steps to Christ*, Ellen White says Jesus was given "to the fallen race. Christ was to identify Himself with the interests and needs of humanity. He who was one with God has linked Himself with the children of men by ties that are never to be broken."[1]

It doesn't make any sense to us, but the trajectory is heaven to earth.

In Genesis 28, Jacob had a dream "and he dreamed there was a ladder set up on the earth, and the top of it reached to heaven. And behold the angels of God were ascending up to heaven to flee from earth, that nasty place . . ." No, wait, "the angels were ascending and descending on it" (verse 12).

The angels were traveling up and down the ladder—two directions—and, remember, the ladder represented Jesus.

Jacob didn't dream a one-way street. Jacob dreamed a ladder with angels going up and down. Jesus isn't just about taking us up to heaven, but about bringing heaven down here. The ladder goes both ways.

The Christian hope is *not*, ultimately, us going to heaven. It's heaven coming to earth.

It is the miracle of Jesus' birth. *Heaven coming to earth.*

It's the Darling of heaven wearing dusty sandals. *Heaven coming to earth.*

It is people healed and given sight. *Heaven coming to earth.*

It is people being made whole and made free, multitudes fed and the outcast included. *Heaven coming to earth.*

It is the dead brought to life. *Isn't that heaven on earth?*

It is the Holy Spirit dwelling in us. *Heaven coming to earth.*

It is the people of God living out the principles of heaven to transform the planet. *Heaven coming to earth.*

It is the coming of Christ, the world made new and the heavenly city brought to the newly restored earth. *Heaven coming to earth.*

This is no longer a waiting room for a departure—an end point—but the beginning of a partnership with the One who will restore all things and renew and re-create all things. Jesus is the overlap, the interlocking of heaven and earth. This is "Thy kingdom come."

I remember learning it as a child. I've prayed it countless times. I've recited it at worship services and in my home. It's printed on a bookmark sitting beside my bed and it's something I plan to start teaching my sons.

"Our father in heaven, hallowed be your Name, Your Kingdom come, Your will be done on earth as it is in Heaven . . ." (Matthew 6:9–13).

It's the prayer Jesus taught His disciples when they asked Him to teach them how to pray.

Your kingdom come, here? *Your will be done*—here?—just like in heaven?

The trajectory is heaven to earth.

The values of heaven. The principles of heaven. The priorities of heaven. Here.

Thy kingdom come.

Kingdom come

When Mary found out she was pregnant, she sang a song that echoed the prophets, declaring that this King would establish a kingdom that lifted up the oppressed and the poor (see Luke 1:46–55). Then, in his first sermon in his home-town synagogue—again echoing the prophets—Jesus pronounced that He was here to bring good news to the poor, freedom for the prisoners, and recovery of sight to the blind. He announced He was here to declare "the year of the Lord's favor," which would have included the cancelling of all debts and the freedom of all slaves (see Luke 4:16–21). In His mission statement, He was declaring a kingdom built on justice, mercy, and equality.

Some might argue that Jesus was talking about the spiritually blind, the spiritually poor, the spiritually hungry. Or that Mary was singing about a kingdom that lifted up the spiritually oppressed. Except that Jesus actually *did* feed the hungry and *did* make the blind see. He *did* spend most of His ministry setting the oppressed free and challenging the systems that marginalized and dehumanized people.

Jesus' ministry was physical *and* spiritual. Jesus demonstrated that

Jesus in Our Practice

the two are not as far apart as we often think. Jesus made it clear by the things He said and the things He did that He really was talking about *literally* setting the oppressed free, making the blind see and the lame walk. These were priorities in His ministry. He really was bringing heaven to earth. *Thy kingdom come.*

He could have still done the incarnation thing, and still died on the cross and done the atonement thing, but why all that healing? Why all that hanging out with the poor? Why challenge the authorities? Why oppose the existing systems and social structures?

Just to declare His divinity? To show that He really was God? Well, why not just use lightning? Why sit on the grass and feed poor people when you could shoot cupcakes out of your hand at a royal banquet?

Why sit by a well and talk to a woman and break countless social codes, when you could fly over Jerusalem and rain fireworks down on everyone, declaring your divinity? Why tell stories about the good Samaritan instead of baptizing thousands of people —or even one person?

Because Jesus *was* declaring the kingdom. What it looked like. What He stood for. All that He is.

> Why sit on the grass and feed poor people when you could shoot cupcakes out of your hand at a royal banquet?

When Jesus gave sight to the blind man, He wasn't just demonstrating a singular act of compassion for *one* man. Every healing miracle was a rejection of darkness and all the things that enslave. Every time He touched a leper and sent them to the priests, He made a statement about all the things that separate and dehumanize: "Every miracle that Christ performed was a sign of His divinity . . . but to the Pharisees these works of mercy were a positive offense. The Jewish leaders looked with heartless indifference on human suffering. In many cases their selfishness and oppression had caused the affliction that Christ relieved. Thus His miracles were to them a reproach."[2]

Every time Jesus spoke to a woman he honored her and pushed back against systems of inequality.

For the One

Jesus made it clear that the kingdom has little to do with worship services and numbers of baptisms, but everything to do with peace, justice, mercy, equality, and freedom. He was bringing the kingdom.

Even when the messengers from John the Baptist asked, "So are you really the One? Or should we wait for another?" Jesus' response was, "You tell John that the lame are walking. The blind are seeing. The hungry are fed" (see Luke 7:18–23).

This is the kingdom. It had already begun. This is the overlapping and interlocking of heaven and earth. *Thy Kingdom come.*

"Your will be done . . ."

Jesus taught us to prayer, "Your will be done on earth as it is in heaven." Imagine the values of heaven, the peace of heaven, the principles of heaven, the community of heaven lived out here on earth. Now. Imagine that!

"Give us this day our daily bread." Imagine a world in which no-one is hungry. There is always enough of the things we need. Enough food. Enough water. Enough love. Enough freedom, voice, dignity. No-one is without. Where no-one is exploited. Where no-one is downtrodden or discriminated against for race, religion, sexuality or ability.

"Forgive us our sins as we forgive those who sin against us." Imagine there is no looking down on each other. We pursue true peace and reconciliation, and we seek right relationships not just for ourselves, but we assist in the restoration of humanity around us. We fear no-one—and no-one fears us. And differences do not result in prejudice. We listen well. And mourn with those who mourn. We put people before policy. Unity is more important than uniformity—not just in our church, but in our world—and there is absolute inclusivity.

An honest reading of the gospels, and focus on who Jesus is, what He said, and what He did can only result in a community of believers who fight against trafficking, who have homeless people in their guestrooms, who are mentoring the disadvantaged youth in their neighborhood, and who are working together to bring the kingdom.

Re-positioning heaven

This does not diminish the wonder, splendor and beauty of heaven or the promise of Jesus' return. Instead, it enlarges it.

Jesus came to be king. Not once upon a time, then one day when. But for all of time—Jesus. All.

Jesus did not come to earth to die just so I could go to heaven. In our excitement about His imminent return, may we not reduce Jesus to a ticket to heaven. He is more. His ministry was more.

Jesus came to earth to usher in a new era, a new kingdom. Where He reigns, where peace, justice, mercy, and equality—the priorities of His ministry—continue as priorities for us, too.

We have been repeatedly warned about wanting a kingdom without the cross, but is wanting the cross without His kingdom just as dangerous? Dare we ask for the "ticket" but say, "Keep the 'love thy neighbor' part because that's just too hard"? Dare we limit the transformative power of grace to only ourselves and our sin, or can we imagine that Jesus did more, is more and wants to do more?

> Dare we ask for the "ticket" but say, "Keep the 'love thy neighbor' part because that's just too hard"?

Grace upon grace!

When we *postpone* the kingdom—living and teaching solely focused on the *getting-to-heaven* part and *Jesus–fixes-everything-then*—we essentially deny the resurrection of Jesus Christ. It's like postponing Jesus' resurrection to the Second Coming. How absurd that we live as if there was Jesus long ago and there's heaven one day in the future, with this long gap where He is silent or distant (or dead) in between. But with the resurrection of Jesus, a new kind of life broke into our world. The rules of the cosmos changed. The power that raised Christ from the dead is at work in us (see Romans 8:11). The power that raised Christ from the dead is at work in this world. Jesus *actually* does things in the world.

We can't just label all the bad stuff as "signs of the times" or simply another point on our prophetic diagrams. Knowing that Jesus will come one day and wipe out injustice and oppression and inequality does not mean we allow it to continue. Jesus didn't want our hope for His imminent return to become an excuse for apathy.

Love does not wait. It will not wait.

Love fights and it stands up and it defends against the darkness. All of darkness. All evil. All injustice. All inequality. All abuse. All oppression.

In any place. In every place. Any time and every time.

Love will not wait. Because Love—Love Himself—is constant. And He is always restoring.

Even as there are wars and rumors of wars. Even as the birth pains become more intense and trafficking gets worse and violence gets worse, so the love defence must grow stronger.

We are not of those who shrink back (see Hebrews 10:39). We are people of Love and "Kingdom come." Love does not store up "Vegemeat" and run to the caves. Love leans in. As followers of Jesus, we find ourselves ever more engaged with our world and its pain.

Jesus is

This is not a "Jesus and . . ." message. This is not "Jesus and justice," "Jesus and mercy" or "Jesus and equality." Because when I read the gospels, I understand that Jesus *is* Justice. Jesus *is* Mercy. Jesus *is* Compassion. He *is* Peace, Equality and all of those things. That's "Jesus. All."

Without justice, mercy, and compassion, it isn't "Jesus. All." It's Jesus-with-bits-left-out. That's the vegetarian replacement version—"Not Jesus."

We can't have the cross without the kingdom.

Because justice is a priority of heaven, I will make it my purpose on earth to stand for justice and speak for the oppressed. *Thy kingdom come.*

Because mercy is a priority of heaven, I will make it my purpose on earth to advocate for the rights of refugees and asylum seekers. *Thy kingdom come.*

Because equality is a priority of heaven, I will make it my purpose on earth to petition for the rights of women. *Thy kingdom come.*

Because restoration and reconciliation are priorities of heaven, I will make it my purpose on earth to repair broken relationships in this world. *Thy kingdom come.*

Jesus in Our Practice

This is how they will know Him. This is the gospel to all the world.

Jesus didn't just tell His disciples once at the end of the book of Matthew to baptize people. He told them again and again throughout His entire ministry to go and *declare the kingdom*—and they were to do this by healing the sick, hanging out with lepers, feeding the poor, and comforting the widows. They were to bring the kingdom.

When we pray "Your Kingdom come, Your will be done on earth as it is in heaven," we are talking about the heavenization of our world. Singing the songs of heaven now. Declaring Jesus' rulership now. Standing up for and speaking out for the values and principles and priorities of heaven now. Our priorities must be shaped by the priorities of heaven as they are found in the life and heart of Jesus. Because Jesus is heaven.

About a week after I overheard my sons' conversations about packing Lego for heaven, I was lying next to Jasper as he was going to sleep.

He whispered to me, "Mum, when will we go to heaven?"

"I don't know, honey."

"I hope it's soon."

"Why is that?"

"Because everything good will be there."

He paused for a few moments.

Then he said, "Tell me again how there will be nothing bad there."

"Well, Jesus will be there . . . "

"Yeah," he added, "and we will have everything we need."

---

1. Ellen White, *Steps to Christ*, page 14.

2. Ellen White, *The Desire of Ages*, page 406.

The One Project blessing

May you be blessed with a spirit of gentleness
and a heart that is tender.

May you be blessed with a spirit of strength
shining within you.

May you be blessed with a spirit of
compassion and care.

May you be blessed with a spirit of courage,
daring to be who you are.

May you be blessed with a spirit of openness,
understanding, and respect.

May you be blessed with a spirit of power and
make Jesus ALL.

Adapted by Dany Hernandez

About the contributors

Dilys Brooks is the associate chaplain of Loma Linda University, where the focus of her ministry is to provide spiritual care for students and staff. Dilys is passionate and enthusiastic about sharing the gospel, as well as equipping everyone to know Christ personally and to become change agents in the world for the kingdom of God. She is married to Dr Delroy Brooks, pastor of the Fontana Seventh-day Adventist Church, Fontana, California, where they are raising their two children, Micah and Matea. Dylis is a board member of The One Project.

Nathan Brown is book editor at Signs Publishing Company, based near Melbourne, Australia. He is a former church magazine editor, a current columnist for *Adventist World* online, and author or editor of 10 books, including *I Hope* and the co-edited *Manifest: Our Call for Faithful Creativity*.

Alex Bryan is president of Kettering College of Medical Arts, based in Kettering, Ohio, and holds postgraduate degrees from Andrews University and George Fox University. He is author of *The Green Cord Dream*, and has previously pastored in Atlanta and Walla Walla, among other places. He is the husband of Nicole Ward Bryan, and they have two children, Audrey and William. He is co-chair of The One Project.

Joanna Darby is an artist, educator, writer, and preacher who is mostly just trying to simplify her life and follow Jesus. She resides in Newcastle, Australia, with her husband Leighton, and two sons Jasper and Rain. She is co-editor of *Manifest: Our Call to Faithful Creativity*. She is a board member of The One Project (Australia).

Japhet De Oliveira currently serves as senior pastor for Boulder Seventh-day Adventist Church, having previously worked as a university chaplain, adjunct professor in youth ministry, youth pastor and conference youth director in his native England. Japhet is married to the former Becky Crooker and they have two sons, Joshua and Jonah. He is co-chair of The One Project.

For the One

Lisa Clark Diller is a historian who teaches at Southern Adventist University in Chattanooga, Tennessee. In addition to 17th-century religion and politics, she enjoys service and activism in her urban neighborhood and ministry in the local church community she and her husband Tommy helped start in 2008. Her academic credentials enable her to talk about history and politics—but her passion is learning how to be part of the kingdom of God, and she loves the friendships and adventures that come with discipleship. She is a board member of The One Project.

David Franklin is currently the co-host of "Let's Pray" on Hope Channel and associate pastor at the Berea Temple Seventh-day Adventist Church. He holds a degree in Business Administration from Oakwood University and a Masters of Divinity from Andrews University. David is happily married to the former Cynthia Ichoya, and they both live and work in Baltimore, Maryland. He is a board member of The One Project.

Tim Gillespie serves Loma Linda University Medical Center as the Faith Community and Health Liaison. He completed his Doctor of Ministry at George Fox University. He has played music professionally—in the band Big Face Grace—and remains actively involved in creating music and supporting local Christian artists. Tim is married to Sara and has three kids. He has co-authored a book with his father, Dr V Bailey Gillespie, entitled *Love Them and They Will Come*. Tim is also a board member of The One Project.

Karl Haffner is senior pastor of the Kettering Seventh-day Adventist Church in Ohio. He is the author of a number of books, including *Destiny, Are Your More Spiritual Than a 5th Grader?* and *Caught Between Two Worlds*, as well as hundreds of articles. He spoke at The One Project gathering in Chicago in 2013.

About the contributors

Dany Hernandez currently serves as the senior pastor of Life Source Adventist Fellowship in Denver, Colorado, and also as an adjunct professor at Adventist University of Health Sciences in Florida. He has previously worked as a young adult pastor, academy chaplain, and worship pastor. Dany is married to Lori and has triplet girls Elli, Gabi, and Tori. He is a consultant to The One Project.

Eddie Hypolite is a pastor, educational consultant and motivational speaker. He travels internationally, preaching and teaching in the areas of urban ministry, leadership, and youth and street culture. His vocational background is originally in the area of residential social work, and he presently serves as the senior pastor of Avondale College Church in Cooranbong, Australia, where he lives with his wife Yvonne and his daughter Rhea. He is one of the founders of The One Project and continues as a consultant to the board.

Brandy Kirstein has degrees in religious education and nursing, and currently works as a lactation counselor. She lives in Erlanger East, Tennessee, where her husband Brennon serves as chaplain at Southern Adventist University, and they have a son, Jax William. Brandy has previously served as a Bible worker and chaplain, and is a consultant to The One Project.

Sam Leonor loves his work as pastor to the students and faculty of La Sierra University in Riverside, California. He has degrees from Southern Adventist University, Andrews University, and is a doctoral candidate at George Fox University. He is married to Shelley Campbell and they have two children, Alexandra and Micah. His hobbies include making music, eating good food, and having good conversations with family and friends. He is a board member of The One Project.

For the One

Timothy Nixon is a graduate of Oakwood University and Andrews University, from which he holds a Doctor of Ministry degree. He has pastored for more than 30 years and currently serves as associate chaplain at Andrew University. He is married to Sandria, a Doctor in Nursing Practice and they have two adult children, Michael and Camille. He spoke at The One Project gathering in Chicago in 2013.

Randy Roberts is the senior pastor of the Loma Linda University Church of Seventh-day Adventists in Loma Linda, California. He is author of *Waiting and Longing*. Randy is married to Anita (Justiniano) Roberts, and they have a son, Austin, and a daughter, Miranda. He spoke at The One Project gathering in Chicago in 2013.

Stephan Sigg is the Director of Youth Ministries for the Inter-European Division, based in Bern, Switzerland. He is also an adjunct lecturer in practical theology at the Friedensau Adventist University (FAU) in Germany. He holds a doctorate in youth ministry from Andrews University and is co-founder of the RPI (Religious Education Institute) in the German-speaking countries of Europe. Stephan is a native of Switzerland, where he lives with his wife Gabriela, a remedial and special education teacher. They have two grown children. He spoke at The One Project gathering in Chicago in 2013.

Terry Swenson serves as campus chaplain and an associate professor of the School of Religion at Loma Linda University, California. He received his Doctor of Ministry degree with an emphasis in the areas of postmodernity, cross-cultural and global interactions, and leadership. Terry is married to Marion and they are the proud parents of four children—Jasmine, Mia, Crystal, and Jared—and are loving their grandson, Ace. He is a board member of The One Project.

About the contributors

Emily Whitney is Pastor for Spiritual Development at the Walla Walla University Church and has served as an adjunct professor in religion at Walla Walla University and Southern Adventist University. She is currently working toward a Doctor of Ministry degree through Andrews University, with an emphasis on Discipleship and Biblical Spirituality. Emily is married to Nathaniel Whitney, a resident in neurosurgery and partner in ministry. She spoke at The One Project gathering in Chicago in 2013.

Mark Witas is lead pastor at Pacific Union College Church in Angwin, California. He has worked as a pastor, chaplain, teacher, and dean, and is author of three books, *Portal* (2014 youth devotional), *Live Out Loud* and *Born Chosen*. Mark is married to Wendy and they have one son, Cole. Mark was a speaker at The One Project gathering in Seattle in 2012.

Join the conversation

For more information on The One Project, gatherings, media and more:
- Visit www.the1project.org
- Like our Facebook page www.facebook.com/the1project
- Join the Facebook group www.facebook.com/groups/theoneproject/
- Follow us on Twitter @the1project